Ben

The LSAT Is Easy

Crush the LSAT with common sense.

The LSAT Is Easy
by Nathan Fox and Ben Olson

All materials, names, and terms in this book are the property of LSAT Demon except where otherwise noted. Nothing in this book should be construed as granting, by implication or otherwise, any license or right to use any of these materials, names, terms, and trademarks displayed in this book, without the written permission of LSAT Demon. None of the material may be copied, reproduced, distributed, republished, downloaded, displayed, posted, or transmitted in any form or by any means, including, but not limited to, electronic, mechanical, photocopying, recording, or otherwise, without the prior written permission of LSAT Demon. Any unauthorized use of any material contained in this book may violate copyright laws, the laws of privacy and publicity, and communications regulations and statutes.

LSAT Demon provides various materials, quizzes, tests, questions, videos, articles, news, and other information in this book and on related sites ("Materials"). Students may not modify, reproduce, share, or distribute these Materials in any way.

LSAT Demon provides information and guidance about law school admissions in this book. LSAT Demon does not make any warranty of any kind, expressed or implied, as to the results that may be obtained from using its Materials. In particular, LSAT Demon does not guarantee that the Materials will improve your chances of admission to law school or that you will be admitted to any law school. LSAT Demon is not responsible for any loss, injury, claim, liability, or damage, including rejection from any law school, related to your use of the Materials, whether it be from errors, omissions, advice, or any other cause whatsoever. You agree to use the Materials at your own risk.

All actual LSAT questions printed within this work are used with the permission of Law School Admission Council, Inc., Box 2000, Newtown, PA 18940, the copyright owner. LSAC does not review or endorse specific test preparation material or services, and inclusion of licensed LSAT questions within this work does not imply the review or endorsement of LSAC. LSAT is a registered trademark of LSAC.

The LSAT is Easy. Copyright © 2025 by Nathan Fox and Ben Olson. All rights reserved. No part of this book may be used or reproduced in any manner without written permission except in the case of brief quotations used in reviews. Educational institutions and libraries may reproduce limited portions for classroom use under fair use provisions. For information, address help@lsatdemon.com.

Front cover designed by Alla Kupriianova.
Interior and back cover designed by Anita Johnson.

ISBN# 9798312789690

www.lsatdemon.com

Contents

Prologue

The LSAT Is Easy   1

Part I: The LSAT Is Easy, If You Let It Be

Chapter 1: The Demon Way   7

Chapter 2: Start With Any LSAT Question   15

Chapter 3: Timing Is Everything… But Not What You Think   25

Chapter 4: Go Deeper On Each Mistake   29

Chapter 5: Focus on the Easy Ones… And They're All Easy   35

Chapter 6: One-Hour LSAT   39

Chapter 7: Don't Skip Questions or Answers   45

Part II: Let's Get to Work

Chapter 8: Logical Reasoning Basics   51

Chapter 9: Reading Comprehension Basics   59

Chapter 10: Argument Parts   65

Chapter 11: Conditional Statements   71

Chapter 12: Closed Question Types   81

Chapter 13: Open Question Types   87

Chapter 14: Word Strength   93

Chapter 15: Types of Claims   99

Chapter 16: Most Common Flaws						103

Chapter 17: Closed Question Types (RC)				117

Chapter 18: Open Question Types (RC)				121

Chapter 19: Reading Comprehension Core Strategies	125

Part III: Tying Up the Loose Ends

Chapter 20: LSAT Writing							131

Chapter 21: Test Day								135

Chapter 22: Admissions							139

Chapter 23: Testing Accommodations				157

Appendices

Appendix A: Closed Question Types					161

Appendix B: Open Question Types					199

Appendix C: Closed Question Types (RC)				215

Acknowledgements								221

Ben Olson and Nathan Fox

The
LSAT
Is Easy

Crush the LSAT with common sense.

Prologue
The LSAT Is Easy

Nathan Fox (Cofounder, LSAT Demon)

What if I told you that a single idea could immediately increase your accuracy and your score on the LSAT? What if I told you that it could increase your confidence and decrease your anxiety? What if it helped you misread less often? What if it helped you avoid getting "stuck between two answers"?

What if it made you faster? What if it improved your ability to predict correct answers and recognize wrong answers as wrong?

What if this one idea would also help you get more out of your study time? What if it gave you back some of your life while making the LSAT fun?

Realizing that *the LSAT is easy* will do all that and more.

What do you think, Ben? Am I overpromising here? I feel pretty confident that we can do all these things if we can just convince students that the LSAT is easy. After 16 years of LSAT teaching, I can boil it all down to this idea.

Ben Olson (Cofounder, LSAT Demon)

You're not overpromising. But I could see many people misinterpreting what you just said.

They might think, "Okay, if I just realize—or believe—that the LSAT is easy, I'll get a great score." That does sound a little unreal.

But after talking with you for years on the Thinking LSAT and Demon Daily podcasts, I know what you mean.

Here's what we want you, the test-taker, to understand:

Scoring 170 won't happen overnight, of course, but it's much more likely to happen and to happen sooner if you fully understand and adopt this mindset—the LSAT is easy.

If you can start to see just how easy the LSAT is, you can start to tap into the skills you already have and immediately unlock questions that were giving you trouble this morning.

On the other hand, when you think the LSAT is hard because it uses words in special ways or requires you to become fluent in formal logic or "contrapositives," you've tied one hand behind your back.

Stop. The LSAT simply tests your ability to read and understand what's on the page.

You've been doing that for years, ever since you started going to school.

You can figure it out. You can read it. You can think about what the passage is saying. You can decide whether the argument makes sense or seems stupid. You can then read the question and answer it for yourself before you even look at the five answer choices. You don't need to be fluent in LSAT jargon, question types, or anything—just good ol' English.

In short, the LSAT tests reading comprehension and common sense.

The magic begins when you start to use—and develop—those two skills, because they are the real skills being tested.

Stop trying to use the "tips and tricks" that our well-meaning but misguided industry foists upon you. Those tips and tricks sound tempting and useful, but they often distract you from the real test that's taking place right in front of you.

Nathan, you agree?

Nathan

Yes. I don't mean that "the LSAT is easy" is some sort of magical incantation that will instantly confer all the benefits I discussed above.

Instead, it's a lesson students will learn and relearn throughout their LSAT journey.

In the beginning, you must accept the fact that LSAT questions aren't arbitrary. Every question has one demonstrably correct answer and four wrong ones. They are solvable. In that sense, they are easy. You just have to slow down to see how easy they are.

Later in your prep, you'll notice that your mistakes largely consist of misreadings. In review, you'll see the correct answer clearly. If only you hadn't misread the argument, the question, the right answer, the wrong one, or some combination. Even advanced students in their final weeks of LSAT prep will occasionally facepalm at the realization that a question was actually easy, if only they'd read it properly. It's a lesson that you will never stop learning.

We hope this book helps you enjoy the LSAT as much as we do. We're fortunate to be able to spend our days working on these fun, solvable problems with students. Students who say, "You make this look so easy" will soon realize that's because it is. It's a thrill to see that light bulb turn on—to see it "click" for our students.

Quick Overview

Nathan

In the first chapter, we'll introduce the LSAT Demon approach. We'll also give an overview of each scored section and the writing sample. We'll share broad information about the law school application timeline and the value of taking multiple official tests.

Chapters 2–7 go deep into the LSAT Demon approach, introducing the philosophy we use for every question, timed section, and test we do. We'll talk about what and how much to study and explain why you should do the questions in order—no skipping and no going back. And we'll make our best case for why most students should focus more on accuracy and less on speed.

Chapters 8 and 9 introduce section-specific strategies for Logical Reasoning and Reading Comprehension.

In chapters 10–16, we'll cover all the Logical Reasoning theory, concepts, and definitions you'll ever need.

In chapters 17–19, we'll do a refresher on Reading Comprehension.

We'll wrap up with our thoughts on the LSAT writing sample, test day, admissions, and accommodations in chapters 20–23.

As always, I trust that Ben will feel free to call me on any BS he detects. And I'll let him offer his final thoughts before taking us into chapter 1.

Ben

Just yesterday, I read an article that used the word "incantation." Based on the context and my vague sense of what it meant, I was tempted to keep reading. But I stopped. I selected the word and looked it up. It's a "series of words said as a magic spell or charm."

Pausing to find and read that definition brought clarity to the sentence I was reading and made a few points later in the article even clearer as they obviously referred back to that idea.

That was yesterday. Little did I know that Nathan would use that same word today.

Although you can't look up words while you're doing a practice test, you can look them up afterward.

Nathan

In a way, you looked up "incantation" in advance!

Ben

Yep. It's one small step in the quest to become, as you always say, a gladiator of the English language. Attorneys are those gladiators. The LSAT is your first step toward becoming one.

We're here to help. If you have any questions along the way, email the world's best help team at help@lsatdemon.com or call them at (703) 787-4007.

Part I:

The LSAT Is Easy, If You Let It Be

Chapter 1
The Demon Way

Chapter Overview

In this chapter, we'll start with a short description of the test. We'll then expand our view to talk about the larger game that's being played: the law school discounting game. Given what we know about law school scholarships (discounts) and how law schools evaluate multiple scores, we'll then talk about the ideal law school admissions timeline, which is longer than most novices tend to think. We'll wrap up by making the case that every student should plan to take the official LSAT at least twice.

What the LSAT Tests

The LSAT is made up of three scored multiple-choice sections, an additional unscored, experimental multiple-choice section used to test questions for future tests, and an unscored writing sample. These sections are added together to create a final score between 120 and 180. Students have 35 minutes per section by default, but testing accommodations are available for test-takers with documented disabilities. More on accommodations in chapter 23.

Two of the scored sections are called Logical Reasoning. Each Logical Reasoning section has around 25 questions. Each question consists of a short passage (one to four sentences), a question, and five answers to choose from.

The other scored section is called Reading Comprehension. It has around 27 questions. Each section is divided into four longer passages (usually around 15 to 20 sentences or 450 words). Each RC passage is followed by five to eight questions, each with five answer choices.

We'll talk about the unscored writing sample in chapter 20. Don't worry about it for now.

Although we'll try to avoid jargon, it won't be long before you're calling these two sections—Logical Reasoning and Reading Comprehension—LR and RC.

RC tests your ability to read dense, often poorly written passages. The questions often seem convoluted but are ultimately straightforward. All they really ask is what the passage says. Chapters 9 and 17 through 19 will offer more on the RC section.

LR also requires you to read and comprehend dense sentences, arguments, questions, and answer choices. In this way, the LSAT tests your reading comprehension from its first question to its last.

The two LR sections test your ability to analyze arguments and short sets of facts. Most of the arguments are bogus, frequently in obvious ways. You will be asked to identify their conclusions, describe their weaknesses, and find ways to make them better or worse. It usually boils down to common sense, but we'll go deep on LR in chapters 8 and 10 through 16.

That's the overview. Ready for a bit of harsh reality?

Get a Scholarship—or Pay for One

As of 2023, the American Bar Association (ABA) has accredited 197 law schools in the US. Over 116,000 students attend those schools. Of those, around 78% receive some sort of grant or scholarship—which both mean "discount."

Only 22% pay full price.

The game's a bit different at the very tip-top of the pyramid. Schools like Harvard, Stanford, and Yale offer only need-based aid. But almost every other law school offers huge discounts to candidates it deems most attractive. How do they decide who's attractive?

Well, it mostly boils down to LSAT and GPA.

If you don't believe us, check out our LSAT Demon Scholarship Estimator for free at lsatdemon.com/scholarships.

Can I still get a scholarship if I'm a good, but not great, candidate?
You bet you can. Applicants with 3.5 GPAs and 165 LSATs are a dime a dozen—but law schools across the country throw money at them nonetheless. Put 3.5 and 165 into the estimator, hit "update," and scroll down until you start seeing money.

You won't have to scroll far. There are dozens of schools across the country falling all over themselves to give this moderately good applicant free tuition to attend their school.

But what if I have bad grades?
A good LSAT can atone for a lot of undergraduate sins. Let's imagine a bad undergraduate GPA like Nathan's abysmal 2.54 and an excellent LSAT of 170. Can this applicant go to law school for free?

Yup.

So then—who's actually paying?
The money to run a law school has to come from somewhere. We're not too concerned about people who can easily afford law school tuition. But we're very concerned about the ease with which any college graduate can borrow unlimited money to pay tuition.

Six-figure law school debt is common, and it's not exceptional to rack up a quarter of a million or more. It's especially dire for first-generation students, who generally graduate with more debt and worse job prospects than do students whose parents went to college.

At the end of every Thinking LSAT podcast, we say, "Don't pay for law school." We don't necessarily mean that you should take this advice literally—it can, in some cases, be worth it to pay some reasonable amount for your JD.

But you should do your due diligence. Every ABA-accredited law school creates a 509 report for each year. These reports contain critical information for your law school decision, including median LSAT scores and GPAs, tuition rates, and scholarship breakdowns. These reports clearly show who the winners and losers are in this whole game. You should look closely at the 509 report for every school you're applying to. Don't be one of those naive students who's footing the bill for everyone else. Apply with your best LSAT score. Apply broadly. Compare offers to one another. Decide on a school that makes sense—at a price that makes sense—for you. Don't settle.

Your Ideal Application Timeline

Most applicants do it backward. They decide when they want to start law school, scramble to meet deadlines, and sign up for the LSAT before they even begin preparing. Then, they cram at the last minute—if at all. This approach sets them up for failure. That's not the Demon Way.

The Demon Way flips this process on its head. It starts by asking a fundamental question: Do you actually want to be a lawyer? Many students rush into law school without understanding what lawyers do, while others assume it guarantees a high salary. But legal practice isn't as thrilling as Suits makes it seem. Most lawyers never even set foot in a courtroom. They just read and write every day. And while Big Law pays well, those jobs are rare, competitive, and demanding.

If law isn't for you, it's better to find out now—not during or after law school. Talk to lawyers in fields that interest you. Ask them about their day-to-day tasks and work-life balance. Apply for entry-level jobs at law firms or legal departments to see legal work firsthand. If you like what you see, go to law school. If not, do something else. As you move through the application process, keep evaluating whether a legal career aligns with your goals. There's no shame in changing your mind at any point.

We're not here to crush your dreams—we want to help you build the right ones.

On the Demon path, we carefully place our best foot forward at each step. We're "GLAD" to do so:

> G: Grades first.
> L: LSAT next.
> A: Apply after you get your best LSAT score, not before.
> D: Decide whether any of your offers justify going.

GRADES FIRST

If you're still finishing up your undergraduate degree, make sure you're getting straight A's. C's might get degrees, but they don't get into Harvard, and they don't get scholarships without putting immense pressure on your LSAT.

We commonly tell students in our classes to take a break from LSAT studying if they have undergraduate assignments or exams to worry about. Don't spread yourself too thin!

If you're getting straight A's and want to study for the LSAT alongside your studies, great. If not, take a break from the LSAT until you've finished your degree. You get only one shot at your undergraduate GPA, and it greatly impacts the price you'll pay for law school.

LSAT NEXT

The LSAT is the single numerical measure that compares applicants on a level playing field. A 3.5 in aeronautical engineering from MIT might have been vastly more difficult to attain than a 3.5 in political science from Fresno State. Schools can compare LSAT scores directly and thus give them a ton of weight in admissions decisions and scholarship calculations.

Most students take two to three months at a minimum to start achieving their true potential on practice tests. Many students take six months or longer. It's difficult to predict who will get there quickly and who will take longer. Scheduling the test is expensive, and it's even more expensive to keep scheduling, rescheduling, and withdrawing or canceling.

So don't schedule official LSATs until you're happy with your practice scores. Take your practice tests seriously, watch your score go up over time, and register when you start seeing scores that will get you into the right school at the right price.

APPLY AFTER YOUR BEST LSAT

U.S. law schools care about your highest LSAT score, and they don't care how many times you take it to get that score.

Students are allowed to take the test five times in five years, with a lifetime max of seven attempts. We've sent students who took the test five times to Harvard and Yale. Only their highest score mattered, and only your highest score will matter.

A single Canadian law school, McGill, says they look at average scores. Everywhere else, the high score trumps all.

Because you're allowed to take the test five times, and your highest score is the only one that matters, there's a huge incentive to retake the test if your first attempt goes poorly for whatever reason. Most people grasp the idea that they should plan for at least two attempts, but we think most students should plan for all five.

To see why, you need to understand the bet you make every time you decide to take the official LSAT. It's a bet that's insanely lopsided in your favor—if you're prepared.

You rarely encounter these odds: If you retake the test and your score drops, nothing happens. Schools will use your previous, higher score to evaluate your application. But if your score goes up, even by just a point, you win—potentially as much as $10,000 in scholarships per point.

So even if you've taken the LSAT three times and gotten some of your best scores on record, if your practice test scores suggest you could do better on your fourth attempt, it's a little insane not to try again. Granted, it will cost you some time and money. Registering for the LSAT isn't cheap. Studying for the test isn't cheap. But these expenses are pennies compared to the tens—and potentially hundreds—of thousands you're about to spend on law school.

Students who shortchange their potential attempts are being penny-wise but pound-foolish.

It takes time for some people to fully embrace what's happening here. So don't worry if you're feeling a little skeptical. We'll come back to this idea again.

Even for those who aren't worried about the cost of law school, planning to take the test multiple times is still the best way to get your best score and thus get into the best schools.

Ironically, the more times you plan to take the LSAT, the fewer times you'll likely need to do so. By planning to take the test, say, five times, you're subconsciously telling yourself that the first attempt is just that—your first attempt. And your second attempt is just that—your second attempt. And so on. This mindset relieves you of so much pressure. As the pressure drops, so does your test anxiety, which then increases the chances that you'll succeed.

In short, most students should let go of their imagined law-school timelines entirely, at least until they're nearing the end of their LSAT journey. Way too much money is at stake. Don't make the tragic mistake of overpaying for law school by $100,000 because you rushed this process.

DECIDE

By applying with your best LSAT score and by applying broadly (to at least ten schools), you'll get the best possible gauge of what you're worth to various schools. Some schools might not admit you. Others will offer you a full-tuition discount and maybe even a stipend. Other schools will offer you a partial discount.

You can compare these offers and even negotiate them. If none of them make financial sense, then don't go to law school, at least not this year. Some people hate this advice. It's as if we're killing their dreams. But law school debt is the real dream killer. Just search for "law school debt horror stories." It's gut-wrenching. And remember, law school will be there next year and the year after that. It never makes good financial sense to pay full price at a mediocre school.

The Demon Way might not be for everyone. It's certainly not for people who are just trying to squeeze out a few more LSAT points so that they can slip in their application by the deadline to please their parents or to leave their jobs.

We'd lose sleep at night if we thought we were helping you line up to pay full price for law school. We want you to take time to realize how easy the LSAT is, to get a score that reflects your true potential, and to apply early and broadly. We can't wait to hear about the amazing offers you receive if you do it our way.

With that, it's time to start our LSAT studies. This, too, is easy. Every LSAT study session can start the same way:

Just do any LSAT question.

Chapter 2
Start With Any LSAT Question

Chapter Overview

In this chapter, we'll explain why there's no right or wrong place to start. All you need is one LSAT question. If you've never done a question before, that will change by the end of this chapter.

The LSAT is easy because it's so literal. It includes challenging vocabulary and byzantine sentence structure, but its questions make perfect sense once you make sense of them. That's all we really do when we study the LSAT: We make the LSAT easy, one question at a time, one sentence at a time, and one word at a time.

Start Anywhere

It doesn't matter where you start. You don't need to go find the "right" LSAT question. You just need to find any official LSAT question and do it.

That could be the first question in any test you happen to have. That could be the last question. That could be some random question in the middle. That could be the question we're about to give you in this chapter.

The point is that it doesn't matter. You will make progress on the LSAT by simply doing questions and learning from your mistakes.

That fact might sound so obvious that it's stupid, but people miss this point all the time. They buy study schedules that include lessons on certain question types followed by lists of questions that they must do over the next three months.

Sadly, those schedules often do more harm than good. They pretend that learning is linear and takes everyone the same amount of time.

But students scoring in the 140s need more time to review their mistakes than students scoring in the 170s. And as your skills improve, your understanding of all question types will improve. In other words, you don't master one question type and then start mastering the next one. Instead, you learn from each mistake, and those lessons help you understand everything else a little more clearly.

TWO PRINCIPLES

To be clear, although we don't care which questions you do, there are two principles to keep in mind as you start doing questions. Understanding these two principles is key because although they're backed by research, they're counterintuitive—so most people don't follow them:

1. You'll learn more from easier questions than from harder ones.
2. You'll learn more from doing different types of questions than from doing the same type.

The Harder Questions Myth
So many newbies want to see the hardest questions first. "Hey, if I can figure out these harder ones," they reason, "then the easier ones will be no problem."

Although that might be true in some cases, the vast majority of questions on the LSAT are easy questions that repeat the same logical flaws. As you build a solid understanding of those flaws, the harder variants will make more sense.

So start with the easier questions and master those. The ideal difficulty level is just above wherever you're at, which is often lower than most people want to believe.

The Same Type Myth
Similarly, newbies want to do the same types of questions over and over. They

want to do 100 Strengthen questions, and then 100 Weaken questions, and then 100 Flaw questions. Stop.

The progress you'll make with that strategy feels good. But the research (and our experience) shows that feeling progress and making progress are two different things. As it turns out, jumping from one question type to the next might feel more challenging, but doing so produces faster results. (See *Make It Stick: The Science of Successful Learning* by Peter Brown to learn more about the robust research backing this approach.)

In short, start with easier questions—usually at the beginning of the section—and don't worry about what type of questions you're answering. Just do them.

SMART DRILLING

To make this process easier, we created Smart Drilling in LSAT Demon. In fact, it's why we created the Demon.

When you drill in the Demon, it quickly learns how good you are at the LSAT. It then gives you questions that are right at or slightly above your skill level. It also jumps around from one type of question to the next, depending on what you need to work on most.

The results have been exciting and motivating. You no longer have to decide which question to do. The Demon finds one for you. You do it. The Demon then tells you whether you got it right or wrong. If you got it wrong or want to understand it more deeply, you read the explanation and watch the videos of Ben and Nathan solving the question. If you still don't understand it, you hit the Ask button.

Oh, and by the way, it's free.

You don't need your computer or this book to get to work. You can access all of LSAT Demon's features on our app.

THE ASK BUTTON

If you drill with LSAT Demon, every question has an Ask button. If you're lost after you've finished the question, read the explanation, and watched a video explanation, the Ask button is your chance to ask your question directly to an LSAT expert. Within 24 hours, you'll receive an individualized response directly from one of our 170+ scoring tutors.

One Real LSAT Question

It's time to turn to our first real LSAT question. We'll start with Logical Reasoning, since it makes up two-thirds of the modern test (2024).

Also, we think Logical Reasoning is just plain fun!

Logical Reasoning consists mostly of terrible arguments. The author will try to convince you of something, and it's your job to tell them why their argument stinks. For now, you just need to know that the trick is to separate the evidence from the conclusion. In short, conclusions are what the author is trying to prove, and evidence is their reasons for believing the conclusion. We'll go into a lot more detail on arguments in chapter 10. Give the author credit for their evidence, but argue with the conclusion they reach from that evidence. Look for ways to say, "Even if I accept all your evidence as true, it still doesn't prove your conclusion because…"

There's not that much to it, we promise.

We'll tell you upfront that this first argument is bad. If you can articulate why it's bad, you'll be answering the question before you even read it. It's fun and easy to do the LSAT this way—welcome to the free-points party.

START WITH THE PASSAGE

But first, we want to give one of the most critical strategies on the LSAT: Start with the passage. Don't worry about anything else. This test is won or lost in the passage. Almost all newbies fail to grasp this point, cruising through the passage and rolling up their sleeves in the answer choices. At that point, they've already lost.

Avoid that mistake by reading this passage slowly, carefully, and with a critical eye. What is each sentence really saying? Stop. Think. Next sentence. You got this.

Test 123, Section 2, Q2
All Labrador retrievers bark a great deal. All Saint Bernards bark infrequently. Each of Rosa's dogs is a cross between a Labrador retriever and a Saint Bernard. Therefore, Rosa's dogs are moderate barkers.

Ben
    Every question has a QR code that will take you to that question in the Demon, where you can access written and video explanations. We recommend you do these questions online, study the explanations, and use the Ask button to get even more help—for free.

The test-writers didn't tell us who's making this pitiful argument. So let's call this chap "Joe," so we have someone to pick on.

Joe lays out his evidence in his first three sentences:

- All Labrador retrievers bark a great deal.
- All Saint Bernards bark infrequently.
- Each of Rosa's dogs is a cross between a Labrador retriever and a Saint Bernard.

We nod and dutifully accept those claims as true. He then dramatically concludes: "Therefore, Rosa's dogs are moderate barkers." (Imagine Joe adding, "That's just science!" for emphasis.)

Do you buy it?

DESTROY THE ARGUMENT

The main thing we're doing in Logical Reasoning is destroying weak arguments. We're saying, "Even if your evidence is true, Joe, your conclusion doesn't have to be true." Here, specifically, we're saying, "Look, Joe, we like what you're saying about Labradors and Saint Bernards, but Rosa's cross-bred dogs don't have to be moderate barkers."

Joe never provides evidence about what happens when mixing two breeds. He just assumes that everything is split 50-50. But Rosa's dogs could have inherited characteristics from either of the two purebreds. They could have inherited the Labrador's annoying bark and the Saint Bernard's awkward smile—or vice versa. We have no clue. If crossbreeding worked the way Joe thinks it does, you'd likely end up halfway between the heights of your mother and father. In short, the idea that her dogs must be moderate barkers just isn't justified.

Here's another argument by Joe's friend and fellow amateur scientist that makes the same mistake:

> All monkeys are good climbers but bad swimmers, and all fish are good swimmers but bad climbers. So this freakish cross between a monkey and a fish will be a moderate swimmer and a moderate climber.

Does that make sense? No. Common sense says we can't predict how such a wonky hybrid would turn out. Maybe it'd become a super predator with superior climbing and swimming abilities—or a total evolutionary dead end, unable to walk or swim. Joe's logic about Rosa's dogs has the same problem.

To be clear, we're not saying that his conclusion is false.

All of Rosa's cute dogs might end up being moderate barkers. Totally possible. We're just saying that—based on the evidence he gave us—that conclusion doesn't have to be true. When any author draws a conclusion on the LSAT, they're saying that their conclusion is proven by their evidence. Sometimes it is. But that's rare. So watch out.

In case you missed it, one starter tip is to get skeptical when you see words like "therefore," which often—but not always—introduce the argument's conclusion. When the author says "therefore," you should say "not so fast."

Now on to the question:

UNDERSTAND THE QUESTION

Test 123, Section 2, Q2
All Labrador retrievers bark a great deal. All Saint Bernards bark infrequently. Each of Rosa's dogs is a cross between a Labrador retriever and a Saint Bernard. Therefore, Rosa's dogs are moderate barkers.

Which one of the following uses flawed reasoning that most closely resembles the flawed reasoning used in the argument above?

This question asks us to find another argument that uses the same bad reasoning. The correct answer will be an argument that is both (1) flawed and (2) flawed in the same way.

20 The LSAT Is Easy

Before you move on to the answer choices, come up with a similar example to the monkey-fish one above. Give it a few seconds. This is a step that many LSAT novices skip. They hurry through the passage, then take a long time evaluating each answer choice without first stopping to consider what the right answer should look like. LSAT experts take their time and calmly make predictions before looking at the answers. Be an LSAT expert.

Did you come up with an example? It will take some effort. But building this skill will help you answer this question faster and destroy future arguments more adeptly.

What do you think of answer A?

A. All students who study diligently make good grades. But some students who do not study diligently also make good grades. Jane studies somewhat diligently. Therefore, Jane makes somewhat good grades.

Stop. Good or bad answer? You decide.

Explanation for A

The first problem we see with this answer is the word "some" in the second sentence. The argument about Rosa's dogs never used "some"—it was all or nothing. So we're already skeptical and moving on to answer B. To be sure, there are other problems. But it takes only one problem to cross out an answer.

Remember that 80% of the answer choices are wrong. Start with the presumption that the one you're reading is wrong. And the instant something about it looks sketchy, move on. You can always come back—but only after reading and eliminating the other choices.

Give it a try now by reading the answer choices below. As soon as you smell something fishy, move on. You'll make mistakes. You might move on too quickly for the wrong reasons. But that's okay. That's all part of the process.

B. All type A chemicals are extremely toxic to human beings. All type B chemicals are nontoxic to human beings. This household cleaner is a mixture of a type A chemical and a type B chemical. Therefore, this household cleaner is moderately toxic.

C. All students at Hanson School live in Green County. All students at Edwards School live in Winn County. Members of the Perry family attend both Hanson and Edwards. Therefore, some members of the Perry family live in Green County and some live in Winn County.

D. All transcriptionists know shorthand. All engineers know calculus. Bob has worked both as a transcriptionist and as an engineer. Therefore, Bob knows both shorthand and calculus.

E. All of Kenisha's dresses are very well made. All of Connie's dresses are very badly made. Half of the dresses in this closet are very well made, and half of them are very badly made. Therefore, half of the dresses in this closet are Kenisha's and half of them are Connie's.

Explanation for B

B. All type A chemicals are extremely toxic to human beings. All type B chemicals are nontoxic to human beings. This household cleaner is a mixture of a type A chemical and a type B chemical. Therefore, this household cleaner is moderately toxic.

This answer looks great.

Type A is very toxic, but Type B is nontoxic; therefore, a blend of the two will be "moderately toxic"? How on earth could we know that to be true? It's possible that the mix could be very toxic or not toxic at all—just as Rosa's dogs might bark incessantly or never.

This is a bad argument, and it's bad in the same way as Joe's.

Even though it's so good, we're still going to read the last three answers. Maybe we're missing something here, and answer B will turn out to be dead wrong. But for now, it's our top pick.

Because we're feeling so good about answer B, our BS detector is even more sensitive than before. We read answers A and B knowing that they had an 80% chance of being wrong. Now we're going to read answers C, D, and E confident that they have a 99% chance of being wrong.

Explanation for C

C. All students at Hanson School live in Green County. All students at Edwards School live in Winn County. Members of the Perry family attend both Hanson and Edwards. Therefore, some members of the Perry family live in Green County and some live in Winn County.

There's no flaw here. If all the facts are true, then the conclusion must also be true. Remember we're looking for a flawed argument. So this can't be our answer.

Explanation for D

D. All transcriptionists know shorthand. All engineers know calculus. Bob has worked both as a transcriptionist and as an engineer. Therefore, Bob knows both shorthand and calculus.

This argument might be flawed in that Bob could be retired and could have forgotten both shorthand and calculus. Still, it isn't the same flaw. There's nothing here about mixing two things together and having a "moderate" outcome—such as Bob knowing a little of each skill.

Answer B is still the best answer by far.

Explanation for E

E. All of Kenisha's dresses are very well made. All of Connie's dresses are very badly made. Half of the dresses in this closet are very well made, and half of them are very badly made. Therefore, half of the dresses in this closet are Kenisha's and half of them are Connie's.

Eh, "Half of the dresses in this closet are very well made"? Do you see the two problems?

To mix the two types of dresses together into a new dress—just as Joe mixed the two types of dogs into Rosa's dogs—we would need something like, "Each of the dresses in this closet is made from Kenisha's dresses and Connie's dresses."

But this third sentence is mixing the characteristics of their dresses ("very well made" and "very badly made") rather than their source ("Kenisha's dresses" and "Connie's dresses") into something else entirely ("this closet") rather than into a new dress.

If you don't see both mistakes, reread Joe's argument, reread answer E, and think about them a little longer. Either mistake, by itself, kills this answer. And that's exactly how the best test-takers move quickly. They move on from an answer at the first sign of trouble—not the last.

We now know that answer B is correct. Choose it, go to the next question, and don't look back.

IMPORTANCE OF REVIEW

It matters very little which question you start with every day. Any question is as good as any other. What's not arbitrary, however, is how you review.

When you miss a question, you must confront the reality that you made not just one but two mistakes. You picked a wrong answer, and you failed to pick the correct one. These two separate mistakes offer you two opportunities to improve. By studying why right answers are right, you'll get better at recognizing how good the correct answers actually are. By studying why wrong answers are wrong, you'll get better at confidently and quickly dismissing wrong answers—you'll learn just how terrible they are.

In short, you should review this question thoroughly before moving on to anything else. Make sure you feel the click.

That means now. Stop. Go back. Do you fully get it? Could you explain it to someone else and help them fully grasp why the correct answer is so good and why the wrong ones are so bad? That deep dive is where the real progress takes place.

With that, congratulations! You've stopped procrastinating and started practicing. From here, we recommend that you start drilling individual questions and timed sections at lsatdemon.com or wherever you do your LSAT studies—but we hope it's with us!

We should shout out the exhaustive video and written explanations available for free at LSAT Demon. Just go to lsatdemon.com to find explanations for the Rosa's dogs question we just did and for all the other LSAT questions in this book.

The rest of this book will continue to outline helpful strategies, but you also need to cover a lot of ground yourself. We'll have plenty of time to develop our LR approach in the next chapters. You don't need to read this whole book before diving in on your own. The sooner you start mixing in your own drilling and timed sections, the better. There's a world of LSAT to explore.

Chapter 3
Timing Is Everything... But Not What You Think

Chapter Overview

New students always ask us when they should start doing timed sections and timed practice tests: Should they study for a week before their first timed section or test? A month? Six months?

None of the above. All students, even novices, should start timing themselves right away.

If this recommendation scares you, you're not alone. Many misconceptions surround timing. Many students wrongly believe, for example, that they should do timed sections or tests:

- to get good at managing their time
- to learn how to finish the sections
- to keep moving, so they don't waste too much time
- to get a score so they can see where they're at

None of these statements are true.

In this chapter, we'll debunk all the timing myths and misconceptions we can think of.

Get Comfortable

At LSAT Demon, the purpose of timed practice sections or tests is to get comfortable:

- Get comfortable ignoring the clock. Most students can't—and shouldn't try to—finish each section in 35 minutes. You only get points for the questions you get right. Accuracy is everything. Don't sacrifice it by worrying about timing.

- Get comfortable calmly, carefully answering the easier questions at the beginning of the section. The first several questions are where you'll score the bulk of your points.

- Get comfortable struggling with the harder questions in the middle. Take your time with each one! The questions get even harder later in the section, so don't give up on these questions too soon.

- Get comfortable taking even more time on the hardest questions that pop up late in the section. These questions require more of your attention, not less. Skimming is never the answer.

- Get comfortable guessing on whatever questions remain at the end of the section. These guesses can earn you a few free points on the test's hardest questions.

- Get comfortable seeing your score at the end, whatever it turns out to be, and immediately reviewing what you got wrong.

- Most importantly, get comfortable learning as much as you can from each of your mistakes.

When you study with us, it's never going to be about pressure, stress, or judgment. It's going to be about staying in the moment and learning from whatever happens.

During your 35-minute sections, you'll calmly answer each question correctly before moving on to the next one. Sure, you'll struggle on a few. You'll take more time on the harder ones because those take more time to solve. If you ignore the clock and take your time, you should get nearly all the questions you attempt right.

At the five-minute warning, you'll fill in a random guess for all the questions left in the section, then get back to work until the time runs out.

Nathan

I was always on team D with my guesses. Ben, do you remember what letter you picked when you had to randomly guess? Not that it matters, obviously.

Ben

Forget team D. It was always team B for me—for obvious reasons. But seriously, it doesn't matter. What does matter is that we picked something without much thought and got free points.

Nathan

Right. Just pick a random letter. By the way, we're dead serious. Even the very highest scorers should be open to the possibility of random guessing at the end of the section. LSAT Demon master tutor Carl guessed randomly on the last question of Reading Comprehension when he got his 179, before heading to Yale!

After clicking your guesses, you'll spend the remaining four minutes or so calmly answering one more question correctly—then one more after that, if there's time. You won't skim these questions or rush through five questions in five minutes. That's a recipe for disaster.

Review Carefully

When time is up, you'll accept your score, whatever it is. It isn't a judgment of your self-worth, it's just a snapshot of one single performance in time. There's lots of randomness in scores, especially when we're looking at single data points. No matter what your score is, good or bad, you'll shrug and move on to the most important part of the process: review.

You'll then carefully review each of your mistakes:

- Why was the right answer right, and why didn't you pick it?
- Why was the wrong answer wrong, and why did you pick it?
- How can you avoid these mistakes next time?

Whether you study with us at LSAT Demon or study elsewhere, it's critical to learn as much as you can from each mistake.

That's why we've created multiple videos and written explanations for every single one of the 10,000 official LSAT questions LSAC has released. We want you to reach those "clicks" of understanding every time you sit down to study. And if our explanations don't get you all the way there, you can use the Ask button to submit a question. LSAT Demon's tutors will respond in 24 hours or less with help.

In other words, it's not how many questions you do each day. It's how many solid "clicks" you make in review. If you review five LR questions today and make three clicks, you'll be way ahead of Turbo Guy who rushes through 30 questions and learns nothing.

Develop Relaxed Confidence

Similarly, racing the clock during your timed sections will only ruin your accuracy. When you master each question through thoughtful review, you'll start to see how easy the questions can be. The right answers are predictable. The wrong answers are garbage. The better you get at answering individual questions, the less time future questions will take.

The point of timing yourself isn't to develop a stressful, race-the-clock mindset. It's to learn to ignore the clock entirely, to do your best on each question, and then to master each question in review.

Every practice section is an opportunity to practice this calm, composed mindset. This practice is how you develop relaxed confidence. The official LSAT will be timed—but by then, you'll have learned to not worry about timing at all.

Chapter 4
Go Deeper On Each Mistake

Chapter Overview

Studying for the LSAT doesn't need to be as difficult as people make it out to be. In this chapter, we'll explain how to study the right way. Follow the steps below, and you'll be headed down the most efficient path to LSAT mastery.

Whether today's your first day studying (welcome) or you've been grinding it out for a year, the formula is simple:

1. Do any LSAT question.
2. Review it until you understand it.

If you just do these two things, you're set. We're not kidding. The LSAT is easy.

Review Until You Understand

The last chapter was all about step one, so let's talk more about that second step. How can you squeeze the most learning out of each mistake?

Too often, students do question after question without learning anything as they go. They do a question, miss it, look at the answer key, say something like,

"Oh, sure, D, yeah, that's a better fit," and move on to the next question. But that's leaving learning on the table.

"Better fit" is just a lazy excuse for not understanding. If you study the LSAT Demon Way, you're going to make real progress every single time you study because you'll be focused on actual understanding.

What does actual understanding look like?

Start treating every mistake as a precious opportunity to learn. The right answer isn't just "the best fit"—it's 100% correct, and it's the only one that correctly answers the question. The wrong answers aren't just "a worse fit"—they are 100% wrong. They simply do not correctly answer the question being asked.

The first step of review is to attempt the question again. It's best to do this without knowing what the correct answer is. But sometimes that's impossible, especially when you've confidently narrowed the answers down to two and you remember which one you picked. If you can, try to redo your mistakes without looking at the answer key.

Whether you get the question right or wrong on your second try, you still need to review your mistake thoroughly. Getting it right the second time doesn't mean you understand the question or why you missed it in the first place.

As you review, remember that it takes at least two mistakes to miss a question. You have to pick a wrong answer while also failing to pick the right one. Investigate both sides of this mistake.

1. Why is the right answer right? How, exactly, does it answer the question?
2. Could you have predicted this answer? Did you even take the time to predict an answer? If not, why not? If you did, what was your prediction? Was your prediction close or totally off the mark?
3. Why didn't you pick the correct answer? Was there something in it that scared you off? Why isn't that scary thing actually scary now?
4. Why is your wrong answer wrong? How, exactly, can it be conclusively eliminated?
5. Why did you pick this wrong answer? Was there something in it that appealed to you? Why is that attractive thing not enough to make this answer correct?
6. When you picked this answer, did you understand what the question was asking? Did you understand what this answer was saying? It should be impossible to pick a wrong answer if you understood both the question and the answer. Wrong answers are objectively wrong. How will you avoid this mistake next time?

See what we mean about going deeper?

It takes two mistakes to miss one question. Experts don't miss LSAT questions, because they refuse to make both of these mistakes at the same time.

Get Help When You're Stuck

Most of your mistakes will come from simple misreadings, and you'll figure out these questions fairly quickly by reviewing them on your own. But other mistakes will come from deeper misunderstandings.

The LSAT is easy, but it's not always easy on the first go. The arguments are convoluted, and the passages are dense. The correct answers are often intentionally vague. The wrong answers do their best to entice the unwary. Sometimes you need a friend. Or a professional. Maybe both.

PREPPING WITH THE DEMON

Getting your best LSAT can literally change your life. It can open doors to law schools you thought you had no chance at. Some of those schools will want your LSAT so badly, they'll let you come for free. Of course, we're biased. However, we do have pretty solid evidence. LSAT Demon has helped thousands of students achieve life-changing LSAT scores. If you're struggling to understand exactly why the right answer is right, or why the wrong answer is wrong, we've got your back.

On lsatdemon.com, every official LSAT question is accompanied by thorough written and video explanations. When you miss a question, take all the time you need to review these explanations before moving on. Many questions have more than one explanation, so you can approach the question from different angles.

Every question in the Demon is accompanied by an Ask button. If you can't reach perfect clarity with the existing explanations, just send in a question— our team of 170+ scoring tutors will respond within 24 hours.

Demon Live subscribers can also attend live classes on Zoom every day of the week. Our students are encouraged to ask questions at any time—showing up and asking questions is your primary responsibility in class. If you're brave, unmute yourself and shout it out. Or if you prefer, you can ask questions in the chat. Either way, we'll sort you out. We've created a vibrant community of LSAT teachers and learners, all eager to help one another reach a full understanding of each question.

If you need to go deeper on a given topic, such as sufficient vs. necessary conditions or Parallel Reasoning questions, we have comprehensive lessons. Our teachers will guide you to these lessons based on your questions.

If you're on a budget, discounted Demon plans are available. Here's a shortlink to information on the LSAC fee waiver, which will get you $2,000 of LSAT and law school admissions necessities for free: lsat.link/feewaiver. If you qualify, upload your approval letter at lsatdemon.com/plans, and we'll set you up with a discounted plan. It never hurts to apply for the LSAC fee waiver—we've had people tell us they didn't think they could qualify who were approved anyway.

We hope you'll sign up and say hello to us. Scores have skyrocketed since we built the Demon. We think we're part of the cause. If you're not sure which plan to get, start with one month of our Live plan. Come to class and talk to us. We'll figure it out together. If Live isn't the best fit, we'll help you downgrade to a lower plan.

You can make an account right now for free to test us out. Our free plan has all of the LSAT material we are legally allowed to offer without charging. You can learn a lot without spending a penny.

PREPPING FOR FREE

With a LawHub Advantage account or a book of unmarked tests, you can study real LSAT questions for free. It's not the most efficient way to study, but the price is right.

The LSAT's correct answers are 100% correct and the wrong answers are demonstrably wrong, frequently in multiple ways at once. If you study the tests intently, digging deep on each mistake for actual understanding instead of just trusting the answer key, your scores will improve. But it might be lonely, and you might improve faster with a study buddy.

Nathan

A study partner is free, and you should try to get one regardless of whether you use the Demon or any other LSAT materials.

When I was prepping, my study partner and I met once a week for coffee to review a practice test that we had each attempted on our own. It worked great, even though we were at different levels. For her, I was basically a free tutor. (Of admittedly low quality at the time. I had no real clue why I'd gotten those questions right!) And it was even better for me, because the struggle to explain questions to her greatly helped me deepen my understanding of the test.

With a reliable study partner, studying will be a little bit less lonely. And you'll be able to get some help when you need it. Sometimes you won't know the answer and your study partner can explain it to you. Other times you'll know the answer and explain it to your partner. Teaching is the best way to learn, so in some cases, studying with a buddy can be better than working with a tutor.

As a general rule, when you're self-studying, don't take too long reviewing any one question. Give it fifteen minutes max, and build a list of questions you don't understand. Bring this list to a tutor or study partner to see if they can help you figure them out.

Ben

While studying for the LSAT, I attended a class in a local elementary school, squeezed into one of those tiny, single-person desks.

Our instructor, Brent, was top-notch. Just as we do now at LSAT Demon, he guided us through several LSAT questions each night, explaining each one without jargon or unnecessary formal logic—just good old common sense.

When I started teaching the LSAT, I quickly learned that teaching is one of the best ways to learn. Explaining concepts to someone else reveals the gaps in your understanding—and that's where the magic happens. Struggling to articulate an idea sharpens your grasp, naturally boosting your speed and confidence.

So find a study partner. Their skill level doesn't matter. If they're ahead, learn from them. If they're behind, teach them. Either way, you both win.

If you've been struggling for weeks or months without making progress, the odds are good that you've been working inefficiently. You've been doing test after test, pulling that 120–180 slot machine lever over and over, hoping for a higher number, fruitlessly wasting your time.

Stop it.

To make progress toward your LSAT goals, just go do one question right now. If you only have time to do one question, that's fine. Go deep on that one question, and you'll have made more progress than if you'd done an entire test and skimped on the review.

Chapter 5
Focus on the Easy Ones... And They're All Easy

Chapter Overview

If you're not sold on our approach yet, we'll do our best to win you over in this chapter. We'll discuss why an accuracy-first approach is your best bet in the long (and most likely short) run. Prioritizing accuracy is key to making the LSAT easy.

No matter where you are in your LSAT journey—whether you're just starting and trying to break 140, or you're already near the finish line and trying to tack on a few more points for your 170+, the only thing you ever need to worry about is the question right in front of you.

In other words, don't try to do the next question until you've mastered the one in front of you.

Are They Actually Easy?

If you're careful, you'll find that the vast majority of LSAT questions make perfect sense and are perfectly solvable. Consider this email we received from a current LSAT Demon student:

> I'm reaching out for some mindset advice. I've been feeling myself really learning in the last month. I got a 167 for the first time after being stuck in the low 160s for a long time. However, I'm finding it difficult to believe I'm doing as well as I am. Any advice on how to talk myself into believing that I'm putting in the work and it's coming to fruition?

That's right—the test has started making so much sense to this student that she has a hard time believing that her success is real.

This uncertainty is common. Once students commit to the idea that they can carefully solve each question, one at a time, the entire test opens up to them. Commonly, they achieve their first perfect section after two or three months of study and ask us: "But that was an easy section, right?"

Our answer: "Yep—easy for you, because you're good at the LSAT now."

Here's the big secret: They're all easy.

A typical section of Logical Reasoning has maybe one or two questions that give an LSAT expert pause. And the expert still gets even those tougher questions right. Maybe we're not in love with the correct answer, but the wrong answers are even worse. We refuse to pick any of those, and eventually we narrow it down to the right one.

Reading Comprehension might be even easier. The only thing the test-makers are ever testing here is, "Did you understand what you just read?" The passage is a collection of all the right answers. The questions, for the most part, simply ask you over and over whether you understood the main point of the passage. Every question has a correct answer that can be justified by information on the page. Again, it's all right there in front of you.

First Things First

The bulk of your points need to come from the easier questions at the beginning of each section.

Many new LSAT students rush to finish their timed sections. They're embarrassed by their resulting scores, and they think their problem is the questions they didn't have time for at the end of each section. But their real problem is that they missed so many of the easy ones in the beginning because they were so worried about finishing in time. Don't make this mistake.

BREAKING INTO THE 150S

It's easier than you think to break into the 150s. Consider this example:

To score 150 on one recent official scoring scale, you need 39 points—an average of 13 points per section. If you devote your entire 35 minutes to just the first ten questions in each section, that'll get the job done.

How? Well, it starts by getting all ten of those questions right—they're the easy ones. Take time to carefully solve each one. Then guess on the remaining 15 questions. Those 15 guesses turn into three free points, on average, because one out of five answers, chosen at random, is right. You'll earn ten points for correctly answering the questions you attempted and three free points for guessing, securing a total of 13 points. Do this for all three sections, and you'll have done less work and gotten paid more—the 150 you've been struggling to reach.

When you can do this, you'll start realizing how easy the test actually is. If you just take your time, you'll start getting 100% of the questions you attempt correct. Then you can think about the next step.

BREAKING INTO THE 160S

To score 160 on the same test, you need 54 total questions correct—an average of 18 per section. Again, the calm approach is the easiest. Do 16 questions with near-perfect accuracy and guess on the remaining questions. There's your 160.

At this level, you start to encounter some of the more challenging questions that appear in the middle of each section. But if you focus on accuracy, you'll realize that these questions, too, are easy. Yes, they require careful attention. But there's only one answer that conceivably answers any question, and the four wrong answers are demonstrably wrong. You can get these questions right if you take your time. Doing 16 questions per section, you're still guessing on all of the test's hardest questions, but your 160 beats over 75 percent of all test-takers.

And you're well justified in looking for more. Let's get greedy.

BREAKING INTO THE 170S

To score 170 (a score achieved by roughly 3% of students), you need about 22 points per section. The easiest way to do this is to be nearly perfect on the ones you attempt. You tackle some of the test's hardest questions at this level, but not all of them. You're comfortable with a few guesses at the end of each section because you're confident that you're getting paid for all the work you do. The questions at the end are harder and require even more time and attention—if you rush, you're sure to fall into their carefully laid traps.

You should consider each next step only after you've built a rock-solid foundation on the step below.

To score 180 (a score achieved by maybe one in one thousand), you need to get virtually every question on the test correct. On the most recent scoring scale, you could make just a single mistake on the entire test and still score 180.

At every level, it's critical that your accuracy is perfect at the beginning of each section. So start there. You don't need to finish. Remember Carl from chapter 3. He guessed on his last RC question, scored 179, and went to Yale. Are you better than Yale?

Slow Is Smooth, Smooth Is Fast

No matter what your long-term goal is, focus on accurately answering the questions you attempt. Otherwise, you'll miss the easy ones in a rush to tackle the harder ones. As they say in the military, "Slow is smooth, and smooth is fast."

If you remain vigilant about your accuracy, you'll eventually have an experience like the one we shared at the top of this chapter. You'll score higher than you've ever scored before, and you'll do it without breaking a sweat. When you do, you should celebrate and let us know, too. We love seeing our students succeed. It won't have been "an easier test." You'll just have realized how easy the test can be.

Chapter 6
One-Hour LSAT

Chapter Overview

In this chapter, we'll tell you how to study for the LSAT in just one hour every day.

You won't be ready for swimsuit season if you start doing pushups on June 1. But if you start doing pushups in January, you'll have a lot of pushups under your belt by the time your first pool party comes around. Rather than trying to cram all your studies in at the last minute, keep it civilized by starting early and doing a little bit every day.

> **Nathan**
>
> Before the Demon, I recommended the same daily study plan to just about everybody: Do one 35-minute section of a real LSAT, and thoroughly review your mistakes. This should take about an hour in total. When all we had to work with was a big stack of tests, this study plan worked just fine. But now that we have the Demon—especially our drilling algorithm—we can be even more efficient in our one hour per day.

One Hour Every Day

We invite you to start with the following schedule. If you have more than an hour, build from this foundation.

In short, you're going to alternate timed sections with untimed review and practice. The exact days don't matter, but the sequence should look something like this:

Monday Do a timed section of LR, followed by an untimed review of the section—focusing on the questions you missed and the ones that stumped you, even if you ended up choosing the correct answer.

Tuesday Finish reviewing yesterday's LR if necessary. Then use the Demon to drill LR questions, carefully reviewing any mistakes as you make them. Don't save questions to review later. If you miss a question while drilling, it's critical that you review it immediately, before moving on to a new question.

Wednesday Do a timed section of RC, followed by an untimed review.

Thursday Finish reviewing yesterday's RC section if necessary. Then drill more LR questions.

Friday Do a timed section of LR, followed by an untimed review.

Saturday Finish reviewing yesterday's LR section if necessary. Drill and review RC passages.

Sunday Drill LR or RC, whichever section you find more challenging. Better yet, drill with "Demon's Choice" to let the Demon target your weak sections in the optimal amount. Or even better, reward yourself for hitting six days in a row by taking the day off. The LSAT will still be here on Monday, ready for you to rinse and repeat this schedule.

This calm, civilized schedule is sure to bring results over time. It accomplishes several goals at once:

- It covers a full LSAT each week.
- It offers timed and untimed practice in each section.
- It allows you to spend slightly more time on your weaker section without neglecting the other section.
- It includes ample time for reviewing each mistake.
- It allows you to do something slightly different every day, so you don't get bored or complacent.

And it takes only one hour per day.

You're not doing five hours straight of a bored, distracted LSAT grind. You're doing one high-quality hour per day. Take this time seriously. Get the most out of it by approaching your timed sections, review, and extra practice with care.

How to Approach Timed Practice

Make sure you'll be uninterrupted for the duration of your timed sections. Do them in a distraction-free environment—ideally, in the same location and with the same setup you intend to use for your official LSAT. Of course, don't let perfect be the enemy of good—or even great. If you can't study in the same place or with the same setup, study anyway. The key is doing the timed section, one question at a time, as best you can. Use airplane mode or "do not disturb" as necessary. Take precautions against distractions from friends, family, colleagues, and pets. This is your time to grow and pave the path for your future.

> **Nathan**
>
> I'm serious about the pets! I've been in tutoring sessions where the student repeatedly had to leave the room to go manage their barking dogs. I've taught classes on Zoom while students' dogs, cats, and even birds have been sitting on their laps, keyboards, or shoulders. To me, that's just not how lawyers work. The LSAT is easy if you give it 100% of your attention. But if you've got a parrot squawking in your ear while you're trying to decipher the LSAT, you're being wildly inefficient with your time. No distractions means no distractions.

Work diligently for the entire 35 minutes without checking the clock. Remember, you're not trying to finish the section. Accuracy is more important than speed. Take your time with each question and solve it before moving on. Get comfortable—even proud—guessing on a few questions at the end of each section. This is the pacing you'll use on your official test, so use it here on your practice tests and timed sections as well.

When you see your score, take it with a grain of salt. Over weeks and months, you'll accumulate data about your test performances. But in the short term (anything less than a month), there's too much noise in the data. You'll have better days and worse days along the way. Don't make too much of them. Instead, focus on each mistake. Learning comes from reviewing those individual mistakes.

REVIEWING TIMED SECTIONS

Treat every mistake as a precious opportunity to learn. The LSAT repeats itself. Your mistakes will too, unless you inoculate yourself from them in your review.

First, redo the question. Do this "blind"—it's better not to know which answer is correct. Can you get it right if you're a bit more careful?

> **Ben**
>
> But this type of "blind review" isn't enough. Getting it right on a second attempt doesn't mean you understand it now. In fact, the vast majority of test-takers get it down to two answers. They debate those two and then pick one. If they get the question wrong, they quickly pick the other answer. Bravo. Of course, it was the other one they were debating. Most points on the LSAT come from seeing the clear difference between the most tempting wrong answer and the correct one. So don't assume all is well because you got it right in blind review. It's a great start, but only a start. Now it's time to roll up your sleeves to figure out why you made that mistake the first time. Remember those six questions you should ask yourself from chapter four. Use them.

Dig deeply into the right answer. Why is it conclusively correct? Why didn't you see that the first time around? How will you avoid this mistake next time?

Dig deeply into the wrong answer you chose. Why is it conclusively wrong? (Many times, there are multiple reasons why wrong answers are wrong.) Why did you pick it the first time around? How will you avoid this mistake next time?

Sometimes, you'll need help to reach a full understanding. Tutoring is expensive, but a study partner or group is free. It's amazing how much progress you can make by teaching and learning from one another. If you study with us, you can rely on our explanations and the Ask button to nail down your understanding on every question. You may also be able to find explanations on the internet. But be careful—some of those explanations might confuse you more than they help. They're not always correct, either.

However you review, don't move on from any mistake too quickly. Review is where the real progress is made.

How to Approach Your Untimed Practice

Intersperse your timed sections with calm, careful practice of individual Logical Reasoning questions and Reading Comprehension passages. Just do one question at a time, focusing solely on accuracy.

Solve each question before moving on. Mistakes should be rare. Take as long as you need to figure each one out. Expect to feel good about your chosen answer—you should clearly see why it's correct. Expect to confidently eliminate four wrong answers—you should notice how each one is wrong for a specific reason.

Since you're solving each question and not picking an answer choice until you know why it's correct, missing a question should be a surprise. Spend as much time as necessary reviewing these precious mistakes. Dig deep, as described above. Rooting out these mistakes is the surest way to achieve a higher score.

If you're not sure what to work on, spend more time working on your weaker section. Don't neglect one or the other—make sure you practice a bit of both sections every week. But your weaker section is where you have more to gain. So lean in that direction when deciding what to do.

No matter your current level or ultimate goal, one high-quality hour is the first step each day.

Chapter 7
Don't Skip Questions or Answers

Chapter Overview

Many prep companies tell their students to strategically skip questions or answers. They're dead wrong. In this chapter, we'll explain why.

Two different kinds of skipping are common on the LSAT. Some students want to skip questions and do them out of order. Others want to skip answer choices when they think they've found the correct answer. Don't do either.

Don't Skip LR Questions

In a section of Logical Reasoning, the questions are arranged roughly in increasing order of difficulty. Remember, most people shouldn't actually finish the sections in 35 minutes. Until they reach the 170s (roughly the 97th percentile), most students will score higher if they focus on accuracy and guess on a few questions at the end. Students who skip questions are, for the most part, increasing the average difficulty of the questions they attempt.

You can't tell how hard a question is until you do it. For example, questions with convoluted arguments but obvious answer choices are easier than they might appear at first glance. Similarly, certain question types—Parallel

Reasoning comes immediately to mind—can intimidate novices but turn out to be formulaic and easy with some practice.

At LSAT Demon, we're not happy getting you into the 140s or 150s. We want to get you into the 160s or 170s. Doing so requires actual understanding of the test. This starts by perfecting the first five questions, then the first ten, then the first 15, and then the first 20. If you can't start running the table on the easiest questions, which always appear at the beginning of each section, you will never reach your potential. Skipping questions is just taking a shortcut to the hardest questions on the test. Simply put: do not skip questions on Logical Reasoning.

Don't Skip RC Questions—Unless You're Skipping the Entire Passage

It's difficult to reach the 170s without reading all four passages, but some students can reach the mid or even high 160s using a three-passage strategy for Reading Comprehension. Disregard this section's advice if you're able to do all four passages with high accuracy.

If you're going to read only three passages, you might consider skipping a passage based on the topic or the number of questions.

On Reading Comprehension, the subjective difficulty of the questions can be affected by the reader's interest in and familiarity with the topic of the passage. Some people really hate the passages about science. Others, like Nathan, are bored by literary criticism—especially passages about poetry, yuck. If this describes you, and you're going to read only three passages anyway, you might consider skipping a passage with a topic that immediately turns you off.

We're not saying to skim all four passages and decide which three you're going to do. That's a waste of time. Assume that you're going to do the first three passages, in order. But you might allow yourself to skip passage two or three if you really hate the topic. This is a one-time, forward-only maneuver. Don't skip passage three, look at passage four, decide you hate it even more, and go back to passage three. If you're going to skip, skip immediately and never look back. Invest every minute wisely.

Don't Skip Answer Choices, Ever

Sometimes you'll be sure the answer is A or B. Maybe it just fits, or maybe it perfectly matches your prediction—or maybe both. You might be tempted to save time by not even reading the remaining answer choices. Most of the time, you'll be right. But once in a while, you'll be wrong. The potential cost of a wrong answer outweighs any minuscule benefit gained by skipping the remaining answers.

Note that we're not saying you should try to twist wrong answers into right ones. We're also not saying that you should conclusively disprove all four wrong answers before choosing one. All we're saying is that you should take a peek at each answer to make sure it's not an even better version of the answer you were about to choose.

Nathan

This happens to me in class with some regularity. I'm reading answer choice B, and it seems to perfectly match my prediction. I say, "I'm 99% sure this is correct, but I'm going to read all five just in case." Sure enough, when I get to C or D or E, I see that it's an even closer match to my prediction than B was—and in fact, there was a fatal flaw in B that I hadn't recognized until E confronted me with a corrected version of what I thought B had said.

If I'd skipped reading C–E, I might have saved 15–30 seconds. But I'd also have missed a question that I ended up getting right.

Ben

I'd like to add that it takes only one word to make a wrong answer wrong. So although you should read all five answers, you don't need to read each answer in its entirety.

I still remember the class where I read the first four words of answer D, stopped, explained how it introduced a concept absent from the original argument, and crossed it out. When I finished my explanation, I asked the students what gave them so much trouble on this difficult question.

Interestingly, most people had been debating answer D—the one I dismissed in four words. I never even entertained its core message. They had read the entire answer, found it tempting, and got sucked into a time-consuming debate between that answer and the correct one.

As you get better at this test, these clear problems in the wrong answers will start to jump out at you. That's how you go faster. You no longer need to read every answer to the end. You might stop after the first four words. But you do need to read them.

The way we go fast on Logical Reasoning and Reading Comprehension is to disrespect the answer choices. We make strong predictions, then, knowing there are four wrong answers and only one correct answer, we expect each answer to be wrong 80% of the time. If it doesn't match our prediction or if it doesn't sound like it's answering the question, it's probably wrong.

On a first read-through, it should take only five to ten seconds to evaluate each answer. The right answer is the one that probably matches our prediction and definitely answers the question. It's the one that makes sense. When you think an answer makes sense, that's great. It's probably correct. But be sure to take a few seconds to glance at each answer choice. Make sure there's not something else that makes even more sense. To be clear, we're not telling you to rush through the answers. You need to understand what an answer is saying before you eliminate it. But once an answer gives you a reason to eliminate it, don't hesitate.

Reading all five answer choices is like having a backup parachute. It takes two mistakes to miss a question—your main chute has to fail (your first answer turns out to be wrong) and your backup chute also has to fail (you fail to recognize and select the correct answer). If you skip the remaining answer choices, it's like jumping out of the plane without a backup chute. It'll work most of the time—but it's rough when it doesn't.

Part II:

Let's Get to Work

Chapter 8
Logical Reasoning Basics

Chapter Overview

Now that we've explained how to approach the LSAT in detail, it's time to get down to business. In this chapter, we'll explain how you can make Logical Reasoning easy.

Success in Logical Reasoning comes down to three core skills:

1. Understanding what you read
2. Making solid inferences
3. Destroying arguments

The problem is that it all seems so basic. Everyone can do all three of these things to some degree, so when students get questions wrong, they often blame other things. "I just need to get faster," they say.

Yes, to get more points, you might need to "get faster." But how?

In most cases, to go faster, you first need to get better at understanding what you read, at making solid inferences, and at destroying arguments.

Don't look for quick "tips and tricks." Instead, focus on these core skills that will make you not only a better test-taker but also a better attorney. That's why we're all here anyway. You got this.

Understand the Passage

The first core skill in Logical Reasoning is your ability to understand the passage. You know that you can read well when you can clearly restate what you've read. Here's the test:

Imagine that you've just read a short argument on the LSAT.

If you can look up from the test and tell your brother, a high school sophomore, what it says—in your own words—in a way that he can understand, then you understand it. If you can't, then you don't really understand it yourself.

It's that simple. Yet people fail this test all the time.

Try it. Here's a real argument from an official LSAT. What is the author trying to tell you? What's their evidence? What about this argument makes it flawed? Read each word carefully, then put it into words that a high schooler could understand.

Test 141, Section 2, Q1
Editorial: The city has chosen a contractor to upgrade the heating systems in public buildings. Only 40 percent of the technicians employed by this contractor are certified by the Heating Technicians Association. So the city selected a contractor 60 percent of whose technicians are unqualified, which is an outrage.

Most of us have to go back to reread what we just read. And as we start to "explain" what we just learned, we end up using the exact same words that the author used. We can't look up from the page, we can't say what we read in our own words, and we can't make it easier for someone else to understand.

In short, we don't fully get it. Maybe we get some of it, but we don't own it. The LSAT gets easy once you learn to own it.

Make Solid Inferences

The second core skill in Logical Reasoning is your ability to make solid inferences. On the LSAT, an inference is just anything that must be true based on the given evidence. Inferences are easy too, because they're common sense. Let's take a look at an argument from a real LSAT question.

Test 123, Section 3, Q6
Jablonski, who owns a car dealership, has donated cars to driver education programs at area schools for over five years. She found the statistics on car accidents to be disturbing, and she wanted to do something to encourage better driving in young drivers. Some members of the community have shown their support for this action by purchasing cars from Jablonski's dealership.

After reading this sentence, you might mistakenly jump to the conclusion that "Jablonski's dealership makes more money because they donate cars."

To be sure, that could be true. But given what was said, it doesn't have to be true. The argument doesn't say anything about whether Jablonski sells enough cars to offset their losses from donations, so that conclusion is not a proper inference. It's just something that could be true.

If, on the other hand, you concluded that "some cars at driver's education programs are donated," that would be a proper inference because it must be true. If Jablonski donated cars to driver's education programs, then not all of the program's cars are purchased.

Put simply, the LSAT will give you sentences. And from those sentences, you can and should make inferences. But you shouldn't be making things up. Only go as far as the facts allow.

At first, some of your inferences might be wrong. But the better you get at drawing conclusions based on what you've read, the better you'll get at answering the questions. The LSAT mostly tests your ability to read and make proper inferences.

All the "Closed" question types on LSAT Logical Reasoning—Must Be True, Conclusion, Supported, Reasoning, and Necessary Assumption, for starters—are simply testing whether you understood the record (the passage) and can choose answers justified by that record.

And even "Open" question types, like Strengthen and Weaken, depend on your ability to make inferences. In those questions, you are given an argument, which has some evidence and a conclusion. The best way to answer Open questions is to figure out what you can properly infer from that evidence and to spot how that is different from the actual conclusion.

We'll unpack all these steps in future chapters. But the point is that making proper, evidence-based inferences is key.

Attack the Argument

The third core skill in Logical Reasoning is your ability to destroy arguments. Most questions in Logical Reasoning give you an argument. And most of those questions require you to figure out what's wrong with that argument.

Every argument includes evidence (premises) and at least one conclusion. The claim that "you should eat red meat," for example, is not an argument because it doesn't give you any evidence. But the claim that "you should eat red meat because it is good for your heart" is an argument because it gives you both a conclusion and evidence for that conclusion.

To better understand an argument, it can help to reorder the premises and the conclusion in your head like this:

- **Premise:** Red meat is good for your heart.
- **Conclusion:** So you should eat red meat.

To be clear, that premise is horrible.

We're not doctors, but we're pretty sure that red meat is not good for your heart. In everyday life, if your friend made this argument, you could tell him that he's probably wrong because red meat is probably not good for your heart. In short, you could dispute the truth of his evidence.

On the LSAT, though, we're asked to figure out what's wrong with the logic of the argument—not the truth of the evidence.

In other words, if you were to see this argument on the test, you should accept the fact that "red meat is good for your heart," even if you're a renowned heart surgeon who has (foolishly) decided to go to law school and who knows that red meat is not good for your heart. That outside knowledge is irrelevant once the LSAT tells you that red meat is good for your heart. "Yes, sir!" you nod. "I believe you, Mr. LSAT."

But even if we accept the idea that red meat is good for your heart, does that mean that you should eat red meat?

No, no, no.

Just because something is good for your heart does not mean that you should eat it. For all we know, red meat could be bad for your liver. And maybe that harm to your liver far outweighs any benefit to your heart. In short, this argument sucks because the conclusion does not necessarily follow from the evidence provided.

Notice what just happened here:

1. Outside knowledge that casts doubt on the stated evidence is useless. We must accept that "red meat is good for your heart." We can't dispute that fact.
2. But outside knowledge that casts doubt on any unstated assumptions is fair game—and even crucial—for analyzing the argument. We can, and must, dispute these assumptions.

- **Premise:** Red meat is good for your heart.
- **Assumption:** You should eat things that are good for your heart.
- **Conclusion:** So you should eat red meat.

"No!" we argued, "you shouldn't necessarily eat things that are good for your heart, because they might be bad for your liver or for some other part of your body." Granted, we have no idea whether red meat is bad for your liver. But as long as that's a reasonable possibility, it's a perfectly fine way to attack this argument. We just have to cast doubt on the conclusion by casting doubt on the argument's assumptions.

Nathan

All this talk about "casting doubt on assumptions" and "spotting assumptions" might panic some students who say "how can I spot something that's unstated?" But it's way simpler than you might be imagining. All we're looking for is common-sense objections to the conclusion.

In the red meat example above, there are several common-sense objections to the conclusion that "you should eat red meat." What if I have religious objections? What if I don't want animals to suffer? What if the thought of eating meat makes me want to vomit? What if eating meat might make me fat? We could go on all day like this.

Don't get stuck thinking that you have to find specific assumptions that the author has made. Rather, attack the conclusion of the argument on whatever grounds you think are reasonable. The more you practice, the easier this will get.

Ben

The LSAT isn't a knowledge-based test. It's a skills-based test. The goal isn't to remember hundreds of objections to specific arguments. The goal is to develop these core skills. If you can clearly understand each sentence, figure out what each piece of evidence proves, and see why that evidence fails to prove the conclusion, you've won. Slow down. Develop these skills. And you'll start to unlock this test faster than most students who are still trying to remember too many tips, tricks, and shortcuts.

Think about it this way: When someone makes an argument, the burden of proof is on them to prove their conclusion. Their conclusion must follow logically from the evidence provided. In other words, given the evidence, their conclusion must be true. Unfortunately, most people don't provide enough evidence to prove their conclusion. They make assumptions, and our job is to spot them.

When you read an argument, make sure to clearly identify the conclusion and the evidence. In most cases, that evidence won't prove the conclusion.

That evidence might partially support the conclusion. It might even support it a lot. But that's not good enough. If the conclusion is not 100% proven, the argument is making an assumption. And we don't have to accept assumptions as true. That's what we're hunting for.

To get good at analyzing arguments, work on the following:

1. Identifying the conclusion and the evidence in an argument
2. Inferring what must be true from that evidence
3. Spotting the difference between that inference and the conclusion in the argument

Now it's your turn. The following is a real Logical Reasoning passage from an official LSAT. Read it slowly. Is it an argument with a conclusion and evidence, or just a set of facts? What inferences can you make? If it's an argument, attack it. How does the evidence fail to prove the conclusion?

Test 135, Section 1, Q5

In its coverage of a controversy regarding a proposal to build a new freeway, a television news program showed interviews with several people who would be affected by the proposed freeway. Of the interviews shown, those conducted with people against the new freeway outnumbered those conducted with people for it two to one. The television program is therefore biased against the proposed freeway.

Text and video explanations and the Ask button are available free for every LSAT question in this book on lsatdemon.com. Go check it out if you want to get deeper on this question.

Five Stages of Logical Reasoning

FOLLOW THESE STEPS FOR EVERY LOGICAL REASONING QUESTION, REGARDLESS OF ITS TYPE:

1. **Passage First**
   - Don't read the question first! This gimmick distracts you from understanding.
   - Comprehending the passage is the first and most important step.
   - If a sentence doesn't make sense, stop and read it again.
   - Restate it in your head in your own words.

2. **Assess the Argument**
   - Does the passage have a conclusion? Or is it just a set of facts?
   - If it has a conclusion, is it proven? Why or why not? What commonsense objections could you make?
   - If there's a conclusion, remember: the author always thinks that her premises prove her conclusion, but they rarely do.

3. **Read the Question and Predict an Answer**
   - After you assess the passage, read and identify the question type.
   - Based on the question type, loosely predict an answer.
   - Your prediction doesn't need to be perfect.

4. **Find the Right Answer**
   - Look for an answer choice that matches your prediction.
   - If you didn't have a prediction or your prediction isn't an option, evaluate each answer choice on whether it answers the question.
   - Eliminate wrong answer choices as soon as they say something incorrect. We don't need to read every word of wrong answers to know they're wrong. Four out of five answer choices are incorrect! We should read each answer expecting it to be wrong and move on as soon as it says something incorrect.
   - Pick the answer choice that best answers the question.

5. **Double Down**
   - If you're unsure about your answer, read the passage again.
   - If you haven't done so already, eliminate the horrible answers.
   - Read the passage again—slowly.
   - Then read the answers you're debating.
   - Compare those answers word by word. What's similar and what's different?
   - If you're still unsure, choose an answer and move on.

Nathan

Unfortunately, most students start in this "compare answers to one another" mode. They're not critical enough in the first place, so they're always narrowing down every question to two or more answers. This might seem productive, on the surface—but it indicates that the student is being far too credulous of the wrong answers. If you spend too much time comparing answer choices to one another, you're spending too much time with wrong answer choices. Stronger test-takers eliminate all five answers on the first pass more frequently than they think two or more answers are good.

Ben

"But, Nathan, I got it down to two answers! The correct one is the other answer I was debating." It's hard to teach a class without hearing this refrain. To avoid this folly, you need to be not only more skeptical of each answer, but also more critical of the passage. When you get a question wrong, it's super common to hyperfocus on the two answers you flirted with during the test. But the fact that you were torn between two "tempting" answers reveals that you didn't date the passage long enough to know what you were looking for when you started reading the answers. Go back to the passage to figure out what you missed. In most cases, a better understanding of the passage or argument will reveal why the most "tempting" wrong answer isn't tempting at all.

Resist Diagramming

When taking the test, we almost never diagram in Logical Reasoning (or Reading Comprehension, for that matter). Maybe we diagram one LR question every ten tests. That's about one diagram for every 500 questions we see.

Practically speaking, never.

Students are often wary of this advice because so many prep companies tell them to diagram any time they see a conditional statement. We'd rather you understand conditional reasoning for what it is: common sense.

That's why, in almost all the if-then exercises in this book, we'll ask you to restate the if-then statement in your head. We want you to gain an intuitive understanding of what those sentences are saying instead of getting bogged down in technical diagrams. We'll go deep on conditional statements in chapter 11.

Chapter 9
Reading Comprehension Basics

Chapter Overview

In this chapter, we're diving deep into Reading Comprehension.

LSAT Reading Comprehension tests your ability to read and understand poorly written passages about arcane topics.

At LSAT Demon, we divide the topics into four categories: humanities, law, social sciences, and natural sciences. But they're really all the same. They're not testing your knowledge of these topics. They're testing your ability to learn about them from the passage.

Other courses teach test-takers to skim, pick which topics to start with, or do the questions out of order. Ignore all these time-wasting gimmicks. In most cases, do the passages and questions in order.

The passages usually get harder as you go deeper into the section. Let the LSAT be easy by harvesting the easier points first. And remember: It's better to carefully finish fewer passages than to haphazardly finish them all.

Engage with the Passage

Our primary weapon in RC is to be a good reader! This means slowing down to make sure that you're engaging with and understanding the passage—especially up front.

You don't have to memorize it, but you do have to understand it. This understanding will frequently require rereading sentences that don't make sense. As you read, react to what you're reading—does it seem reasonable? Or is it a little strange? What part of it is strange? What part of it don't you understand? Try to predict where the author is going next after each sentence.

Remember those bumper stickers that say, "If you're not outraged, you're not paying attention"? On RC, we say, "If you're not reacting, you're not paying attention." What's that mean?

Learn the Author's Opinion

Some passages are purely informative. The author isn't staking out a position, just relaying the facts or positions of others. But more often than not, the author has some agenda. They'll try to persuade you to their side. They'll subtly (or not-so-subtly) agree or disagree with the positions they're presenting. This is the author's opinion. Be hungry for it. When the author says "Perez says X," immediately ask, "Okay, but what do you think about it, author? Why are you wasting my time with Perez's opinion? I want yours!"

If you engage with the passage, you'll likely glean the main point as you read. The main point will not necessarily be one sentence in the passage. It will emerge over time, often not until the last paragraph.

Keep asking the author: Why are you wasting my time? What's your point?

Restate the Main Point

When you finish reading the passage, restate the main point in your own words before answering the questions.

If you're unsure of what the author was trying to prove, quickly scan the passage from top to bottom. This will help you see the big picture. Restating might take some time—but it will help you go faster in the questions.

You want a concise summary that captures what the author is specifically trying to prove or convey. The topic isn't enough. Don't stop at "what"—follow through all the way to "what about it?" The bad example below stops way too short:

- **Bad**: The passage is about how tigers fight for food.
- **Better**: Many biologists think tigers fight over food only when it's scarce. But tigers fight even when there's lots of food. It helps them establish dominance and avoid future conflicts.

They're All Must Be Trues

When in doubt, on Reading Comprehension, we should assume the question is simply asking, "Given what the passage says, what must be true?" When answering a Must Be True question, pick the answer that has direct support from the passage. Being dull and boring never makes an answer wrong—in fact, dull and boring is exactly what we want.

Step into the test-makers' shoes for a moment. The LSAT contains a section called "Reading Comprehension." What, as the test-maker, do you intend to test here?

Are you looking to examine an applicant's command of logic and argumentation? No, you do that on Logical Reasoning.

On Reading Comprehension, you're simply testing an applicant's ability to understand what they've read. But you get bored asking, "Which one of these five does the passage say?" So instead, you write questions like these:

1. Which one of the following most accurately expresses the main point of the passage?
2. Which one of the following is most analogous to the literary achievements that the author attributes to Dove?
3. According to the passage, in the U.S. there is a widely held view that _____
4. The author's attitude toward the deep rift between poetry and fiction in the U.S. can be most accurately described as one of _____
5. In the passage, the author conjectures that a cause of the deep rift between fiction and poetry in the United States may be that _____
6. In the context of the passage, the author's primary purpose in mentioning Dove's experience in Germany (last sentence of the third paragraph) is to _____

7. It can be inferred from the passage that the author would be most likely to believe which one of the following?

8. If this passage had been excerpted from a longer text, which one of the following predictions about the near future of U.S. literature would be most likely to appear in that text?

These are the eight questions from the first passage of Test 123, by the way.

Are all these questions Must Be Trues? Well, let's look at each one:

1. **Which one of the following most accurately expresses the main point of the passage?**

    Yep. Main Point questions are a subset of Must Be True. The correct answer has to come straight out of the passage. It can use synonyms, of course, but the correct answer has to say something that the passage actually says—or else it's automatically wrong.

2. **Which one of the following is most analogous to the literary achievements that the author attributes to Dove?**

    Tricky, but yes. If we're looking for something "analogous" to what the author says about Dove's literary achievements, we start with, "Well, what does the author say about Dove's literary achievements?" Maybe the passage says that Dove was able to write books while also being named after a brand of chocolate. If that's what it says, then something analogous to that might be, "Hershey wrote a book of poetry" or, "Toblerone wrote a treatise on tort law." Point is, we start with what the passage actually says, then we find something analogous to that.

3. **According to the passage, in the U.S. there is a widely held view that _____**

    For sure. Note the first three words here: "according to the passage." If they're looking for something that's "according to the passage," then we'd better pick an answer that's straight out of the passage. The test is literal.

4. **The author's attitude toward the deep rift between poetry and fiction in the U.S. can be most accurately described as one of**

    Yep. The author's attitude is not something we imagine or invent. They're not asking us to read between the lines; they're asking us to read the lines themselves. Before looking at the answer choices, paraphrase what the author says about the rift between fiction and poetry in the U.S. If the author says the rift is "unfortunate," then the correct answer has to say that—or a similarly negative synonym. If the author says the rift is "beneficial," then the correct answer has to say exactly that—or a similarly positive synonym. If the author says the rift is "mysterious" or "widening" or "deep," then that's what the correct answer will say.

5. **In the passage, the author conjectures that a cause of the deep rift between fiction and poetry in the United States may be that _____**

   Yes. Here, the test-maker is getting fancy with the verb "conjectures," but all they really mean is "says." They want to know whether we understand the passage (and whether we can figure out that "conjectures," in this context, means "says"). The correct answer needs to be lifted straight out of the passage.

6. **In the context of the passage, the author's primary purpose in mentioning Dove's experience in Germany (last sentence of the third paragraph) is to _____**

   Yes. Why does the author bring up Dove's experience in Germany? Well, what does the passage say about Dove's experience in Germany? Did Dove learn about the wonders of German chocolate cake and gain critical inspiration for whatever chocolate-themed literary achievements followed? Well, then, that's the answer.

7. **It can be inferred from the passage that the author would be most likely to believe which one of the following?**

   Yes, yes, yes! This formulation of a Reading Comprehension question is particularly vexing to LSAT novices, who take the phrases "it can be inferred" and "would be most likely to believe" as invitations to speculate. They are not. "It can be inferred" means "it must be true," and "most likely to believe" means "they say this." The most important part of this question is the three-word phrase that novices tend to ignore: "from the passage." They're not looking for us to read tea leaves here or make anything up. They want us to answer the question based on what the author actually says in the passage.

8. **If this passage had been excerpted from a longer text, which one of the following predictions about the near future of U.S. literature would be most likely to appear in that text?**

   Well, this is another weird one—but yes. They can't ask us to magically invent parts of a "longer text" that we haven't read and that might not even exist. Rather, they want to know whether we understand the parts that we have, in fact, read. What does the author say about the current state of U.S. literature? How is it currently changing? The correct answer, if we're making a prediction about the "near future," is going to be the present state of U.S. literature, modified by whatever current changes are already happening, as described by the passage. That's it.

We picked this passage at random, but it's not surprising that all eight of the questions turn out to be some form of Must Be True. The test-makers do throw in a Strengthen or Weaken question from time to time. But when they're asking us for the main point, primary purpose, author's attitude, or any of the quirky questions posed above, they're really just testing whether we understand the passage in front of us. When in doubt: Must Be True.

So, putting on our Must Be True hat, how do we know when we've found the correct answer for each question?

Put bluntly, the correct answer is correct because it's what the passage says. We should be able to predict the answer half the time or more if we stop and think about each question before blundering ahead into the answer choices.

If we narrow it down to two—which shouldn't happen often, because the right answers are very right and each wrong answer is very wrong, often for multiple reasons—we should lean toward answers that are boring, obvious, vague, or restrained. Those answers are easier to prove and, thus, more likely to be correct. We should be extra suspicious of answers that are too specific or decisive or that add anything new, different, or extra. Those answers are harder to prove and, thus, almost always wrong.

Conclusion

The Reading Comprehension component of the LSAT is easy, if you let it be, because the test-makers always give you the evidence you need to justify the answers you're picking. You can make it hard on yourself by reading too fast or panicking about unfamiliar (often science-related) topics. Let it be easy! Take the time to read carefully, and remember that they're testing your reading, not your knowledge. It's the LSAT's most straightforward section.

Chapter 10
Argument Parts

Every argument has at least one premise and one conclusion:

1. A premise is a piece of evidence that the author uses to support her conclusion.
2. A conclusion is a claim that the author tries to support with at least one premise.

Imagine a bribery case. Let's say the prosecution has video footage of the accused, a well-known politician, walking away from a powerful lobbyist with a suitcase of cash. $10,000 to be exact. From there, the prosecution will try to convince a jury that the accused politician took the money and agreed to help the lobbyist—a good ol' felony.

Here's the fun and easy part. You get to object!

Don't object to the evidence itself. Just explain why the evidence doesn't justify the conclusion.

Simply point out all the ways that the evidence doesn't force us to conclude that the politician committed a felony. Maybe the politician thought the lobbyist was simply returning his suitcase. He had no clue it was filled with cash. Or maybe the politician was working with the FBI to catch this lobbyist before she bribed yet another official.

And don't stop there! Even if the politician did take the money and didn't tell anyone, does that always justify a felony conviction? What if the lobbyist were threatening to set off a bomb or some other drastic measure, and the politician was trying to prevent that tragedy?

When you see an argument on the LSAT, it's probably bogus. The LSAT gets fun, easy, and predictable when you learn how to attack these bogus arguments.

Premises

Premises are facts that support a conclusion. Treat premises as evidence and accept them as true regardless of whether they are true in the real world.

PREMISE INDICATORS

"Because," "since," and "for" almost always come before a premise.

In the two examples below, the premise is underlined:

1. The world is getting warmer because <u>atmospheric CO_2 is increasing</u>.
2. Because <u>atmospheric CO_2 is increasing</u>, the world is getting warmer.

In both cases, the conclusion is nearby. Whether the conclusion comes before or after the word "because" in these two sentences is just a matter of style; it does not change the fact that "because" comes right before the premise.

Conclusions

There are two types of conclusions:

The main conclusion is the main point. It's the overarching point that the author is trying to prove. If an argument has only one conclusion, then it is the main conclusion. If it has two or more conclusions, then the main conclusion is the conclusion that is supported by the other conclusions in the argument. It doesn't have to be last; it can appear anywhere in the argument.

An intermediate conclusion is a conclusion that supports the main conclusion. It's a conclusion because it is supported by a premise. But it also acts as a premise because it supports the main conclusion. When a statement serves both these functions, the LSAT calls it an "intermediate conclusion."

> **Nathan**
> In the bribery case above, "should be convicted of a felony" is the main conclusion. This is ultimately what the prosecution wants

to prove. (Not just prove a bribe took place, but also convict the politician of a felony.)

Ben

Yes, "the politician accepted a bribe" is an intermediate conclusion. There is evidence to support it (the video footage), so it's a conclusion. But it's also used as evidence to support the felony conviction. So it's not the ultimate conclusion, just an intermediate one.

ANOTHER EXAMPLE

Premise: Obama is smart.
Intermediate Conclusion: So he will make good book recommendations.
Main Conclusion: So you should follow him on Instagram.

Although you must accept premises as true on the LSAT, conclusions—both intermediate and main—are up for debate. Why can't smart people recommend bad books, or not recommend books at all? The intermediate conclusion is suspect. And so is the ultimate conclusion. Even if we grant that Obama does make good book recommendations, how does that prove anyone should follow him on Instagram? Maybe he doesn't recommend books there. Or maybe social media is evil.

Accept the evidence, but always argue with the conclusions.

CONCLUSION INDICATORS

Please don't try to memorize a list of indicators, but these words can sometimes help us organize our understanding of an argument.

The words "therefore," "thus," and "so," for example, always come after a premise and before a conclusion. In the two sentences below, the premises are italicized and the conclusions are underlined:

George is always late, **so** he'll probably be fired.
Frogs are dying all around the world. **Thus**, we must act now.

Here are the three most common mistakes students make with "therefore," "thus," and "so":

1. Forgetting that they always introduce a conclusion
2. Forgetting that they always come after a premise
3. Forgetting that the conclusion could be either an intermediate conclusion or the main conclusion

The words "therefore," "thus," and "so" by themselves do not necessarily introduce the main conclusion. You must look to other clues in the argument to decide whether the conclusion they introduce is the main conclusion or an intermediate conclusion.

OPINIONS

Although every argument has to have at least one premise and at least one conclusion, you might also see an opinion from other people or a concession from the author.

When an author cites someone else's opinion, their main conclusion will often disagree with that opinion. When this happens, the other person's opinion isn't a premise. But the fact that they hold that opinion is a premise.

Here, the opinion of others—which is introduced by the phrase "most people believe that"—is underlined, the conclusion is bolded, and the premise is italicized:

> Most people believe that <u>life has meaning</u>. **But they're wrong**. *Meaning is illusory.*

OPINION INDICATORS

The phrases "many scientists argue that," "most scholars agree that," and "it is assumed that" all introduce the opinions of other people.

Although the author can agree with these opinions, in most arguments on the LSAT, the author cites these other people to tell us why they're wrong in some way. In this example, the opinion is underlined:

> Newt Gingrich claims that <u>we should create a colony on the moon</u>. But this is a bad idea because, in this economy, we don't have the resources to fund it.

CONCESSIONS

A concession is a claim or statement that weakens the argument's conclusion. Arguments often include concessions, even though they weaken the conclusion, to prevent an anticipated counterargument. Here, the concession is underlined, the conclusion is bolded, and the premise is italicized:

> Although <u>it costs more</u>, **we should buy this car** because *it will last longer.*

CONCESSION INDICATORS

The words and phrases "although," "even though," and "despite" almost always introduce concessions. In this example, the concession is underlined:

> Although <u>a few senators like Newt's plan</u>, his plan will not be adopted by NASA. It's already planning to go to Mars, and it doesn't have the funding to do both.

Read the following argument from an official LSAT, grant the author's evidence, but object to the conclusion.

Test 123, Section 2, Q9
Although video game sales have increased steadily over the past 3 years, we can expect a reversal of this trend in the very near future. Historically, over three quarters of video games sold have been purchased by people from 13 to 16 years of age, and the number of people in this age group is expected to decline steadily over the next 10 years.

Got it? Are you sure? Can you explain it to a high schooler in your own words? If not, go back and read it again slower. There's no shame in rereading. It's a habit LSAT experts rely on. Remember, slow is smooth and smooth is fast. Here's your quiz:

1. What's the conclusion of the argument?
2. What are the author's premises?
3. Is this a good argument (perfect) or a bad argument (flawed)?
4. If you think it's a bad argument, how is it flawed?

Ready for the answers?

1. The conclusion is at the end of the first sentence: "We can expect a reversal of this trend in the very near future." This is what the author is trying to prove.
2. There are two premises in this argument: "Historically, over three quarters of video games sold have been purchased by people from 13- to 16 years of age," and "The number of people in this age group is expected to decline steadily over the next 10 years."
3. This is a bad argument, the evidence doesn't prove the conclusion to be true.
4. This argument tells us what has happened historically in video game sales, but not what's happening right now or what will happen in the future. The fact most video games have historically been purchased by 13- to 16-year-olds doesn't mean that they

will continue to dominate the market. What if the current 13- to 16-year-olds get hooked on video games and keep buying them after they turn 17? If that happened, we could easily see video game sales stay the same or increase in the near future.

If you don't quite get it, it's okay, just go back and try again. If you still don't feel like you're getting it, go to lsatdemon.com and make a free account. You can search for this question and watch our explanation videos.

Chapter 11
Conditional Statements

Even This Part's Easy

Nothing confuses new LSAT students more than the way crusty old LSAT companies talk about conditional reasoning. Unless this is the first book you've read about the LSAT, you've probably already burned out a few thousand brain cells trying to decipher LSAT instruction that sounds like this:

> "The sufficient condition requires the necessary condition, and the necessary condition is the one, without which, the sufficient condition cannot obtain. And when we consider the contrapositive of the conditional, we see that the negation of the necessary condition now becomes its own sufficient condition for the former sufficient condition, negated, to become necessary."

Yowza! The statement above might be logically valid, but it is in no way helpful to any actual LSAT student. Sadly, circular definitions abound when we try to talk about this stuff in the abstract.

Meanwhile, the truth is nothing but common sense. Conditionals are just if-then statements. We deal with them in everyday life. Here's a conditional statement, drawn from real life:

> "If you're driving a Ferrari, you're driving a car."

Even a sixth grader knows that this doesn't mean that if you're driving a car, you're driving a Ferrari. (Hondas and Toyotas are a thing.)

The sixth grader also knows that it doesn't mean that if you're not driving a Ferrari, you're not driving a car. (Because of those same Hondas and Toyotas, which are still a thing.)

This same sixth grader also knows that it does mean that if you're not driving a car, you're not driving a Ferrari. Duh!

If you take away nothing more from this chapter, we hope you'll believe us when we say that this is mostly a matter of common sense. Whenever you start getting lost in the weeds with lessons that focus too much on heavy-handed theory about conditional statements, just consider a real-world example and remember: The LSAT is easy. We'll dig deeper below and cover a few nuances. But there's not much more to it than that.

Nathan

When I started my LSAT business way back in 2009, I fell into the trap of starting the first night of every class with a conditional reasoning lesson. I think I did a pretty good job of explaining everything in common-sense terms, but it was a mistake to give conditional reasoning so much early attention. There's a reason we've relegated this stuff to the middle of this book. It's all just common sense! And it's easier to learn in the context of real LSAT questions. Even if you ignore the rest of this chapter, you'll encounter all these issues by simply working your way through LSAT questions, sections, and tests. If you want to skip the theory, be my guest. Ben, do you feel the same way?

Ben

I agree that it's easier to learn about if-then statements and conditional reasoning through examples, which are littered throughout the test. I also think the little context we provide here can help students better understand those examples over time. In our experience, most people will read this chapter, get some insights, and start to recognize these concepts on the test. But they'll benefit even more when they return to this chapter in two months, after trying to answer scores of real LSAT questions that test these concepts. That experience will give this chapter even more clarity.

Some Definitions

A "conditional statement" is just an if-then statement like this one:

If you drink that poison, then you will get sick.

The if-clause is called the "sufficient condition." The then-clause is called the "necessary condition."

In the example above, the if-clause is the sufficient condition because it guarantees that the then-clause will happen. "Sufficient" just means "enough." You don't need anything else. If you drink that poison, then—at least according to this rule—it's enough to guarantee you'll get sick.

In real life, we might think of cases when people drink the poison and don't get sick. (And in fiction! In *The Princess Bride,* Westley uses his immunity to poison to defeat Vizzini in a battle of wits.) There are always exceptions in movies and in life. But when you read an if-then statement on the LSAT, you have to take it at its word. It didn't say that you *might* get sick or that *most* people get sick; it said that you *will* get sick.

It doesn't even matter if you take some amazing medicine right after you drink the poison. According to the rule, you are going to get sick. It's guaranteed to happen. Sure, the medicine might lessen the pain or even shorten the sickness. But if the if-clause is triggered, then that then-clause has to happen.

That's why the then-clause is called the necessary condition. Simply put, it must happen if the if-clause happens. You must get sick if you drink that poison.

Notice, however, that the reverse is not true. If you get sick, we can't say for sure that you drank the poison. You certainly could have. But you might have gotten sick for some other reason (the flu, one too many glasses of wine, a crazy Uber driver).

In other words, the then-clause isn't called the sufficient condition because it doesn't guarantee that the if-clause happened. For the same reason, the if-clause isn't called the necessary condition because it doesn't have to happen when the then-clause happens.

In short, the if-clause is the "sufficient condition" and the then-clause is the "necessary condition." If nothing else, remember those two names.

Hidden Conditionals

So far, we've looked only at conditional statements that use the words if and then. These conditional statements, not surprisingly, are easy to spot. But most conditional statements on the LSAT use other words to create the sufficient and necessary conditions.

But before we get into those words, we need to review some basic grammar.

Our goal here isn't to be the grammar Gestapo. So if you take issue with the way we explain some things, we apologize. The point isn't to master grammar per se, but to understand a few grammar-related ideas that can help you break down sentences and spot hidden conditional statements.

Although there are different ways to break down sentences, let's keep it simple by sticking with the traditional view. That's all we need for the LSAT at least.

According to that view, every sentence has a subject and a predicate. In simple terms, the "subject" is the actor of the sentence, and the "predicate" is what that actor is doing.

In the following sentence, for example, "cars" is the subject, and "go fast" is the predicate. We're talking about "cars," and we're saying that they "go fast."

<u>Cars</u> go fast.

In other words, everything before the verb is the subject. The verb and everything after it is the predicate.

But when most people start talking about the "subject," they're actually thinking about the "simple subject," which is not always the same. On the test, you want to focus on the entire subject, also known as the "complete subject." In the next sentence, for instance, "cars" is the simple subject and "red cars" is the complete subject:

<u>Red **cars**</u> go fast.

To be sure, this sentence does say something about cars. But it's really talking about red cars, which is a smaller group of things. It doesn't tell us anything about green cars, for example. So although it's helpful to identify the simple subject as "cars," it's more helpful to identify the complete subject as "red cars." That is the real "subject" of the sentence.

What's the complete subject in this sentence?

Cars that have four doors go fast.

The simple subject again is "cars," but the complete subject is "cars that have four doors." Like before, this sentence is not talking about cars in general. It's only talking about cars that have four doors. So that's what you want to focus on.

To find the complete subject, look for words that modify the simple subject. These words can come right before or after the simple subject. Here are several:

- adjectives, such as "*red* cars"
- "that" phrases, such as "cars *that have four doors*"

- "who" phrases, such as "students *who sleep in*"
- "of" phrases, such as "cars *of a previous generation*"
- "in" phrases, such as "cars *in Palo Alto*"
- "with" phrases, such as "cars *with driver-side airbags*"

This isn't a list for you to memorize and call upon while doing actual LSAT questions. The point of this list is to demonstrate a variety of ways to modify a subject. There are other phrases that modify the simple subject and thus become part of the complete subject. But the six above are some of the more common ones.

By the way, the complete subject can be rather lengthy, especially on the LSAT. It's one way of making the test harder. In general, the more modifiers you add to the simple subject, the more you limit what you're talking about.

In each sentence below, we've underlined the complete subject:

<u>Red **cars**</u> go fast.
<u>Red **cars** that have four doors</u> go fast.
<u>Red **cars** that have four doors and driver-side airbags</u> go fast.
<u>Red **cars** that have four doors and driver-side airbags in Palo Alto</u> go fast.

In each case, by adding one more modifier, we narrow the group of things that we're talking about. "Red cars that have four doors and driver-side airbags," for instance, is a smaller group than "red cars."

Technically, just to be 100% accurate, they could be the same size if all red cars happen to have four doors and driver-side airbags. But assuming that isn't true, the group "red cars" is larger. Possibly much larger.

Put into if-then statement form, here's how the previously listed hidden conditionals would look:

If it's a red car, then it goes fast.
If it's a red car with four doors, then it goes fast.
If it's a red car with four doors and driver-side airbags, then it goes fast.
If it's a red car with four doors and driver-side airbags in Palo Alto, then it goes fast.

In short, when you're identifying the complete subject, make sure to include everything that modifies the subject. Otherwise, you might mistakenly think the sentence is talking about a larger group of things than it actually is.

To help yourself identify the complete subject, and not just part of it, ask yourself a yes-or-no question like this one:

Do _____ go fast?

Whatever you feel compelled to put in that blank slot is your complete subject. It's what you're talking about.

Contrapositives are Easy, Too

It's hard to avoid hearing about "contrapositives" when you start studying for the LSAT. But there's no need to spend valuable time going down this rabbit hole. Here's a quick, easy breakdown of what they are and why you don't need to draw them out on the LSAT.

Nathan

I'm fairly certain that the word "contrapositive" has never actually appeared on an LSAT. That's not to say that it never will; I just don't think it ever has. Other LSAT books criminally overuse this word in their lessons and explanations. I want you to understand it, but I don't want you to perseverate on it. Remember: The LSAT is easy. This is all just common sense.

Ben

Some people trace the term "contrapositive" back to an 1847 book by the English mathematician Augustus De Morgan. And they tend to be of about as much use as that knowledge. But I agree. I've never seen it on the LSAT. Let's dive in.

WHAT'S A CONTRAPOSITIVE?

A contrapositive is an if-then statement that follows from another if-then statement. In other words, if an if-then statement is true, then its contrapositive is another if-then statement that is also true. You can determine the contrapositive by switching and negating the sufficient and necessary conditions of the first if-then statement.

Enough jargon, here's a simple example:

If it's raining, then the grass is wet.
Contrapositive: If the grass isn't wet, then it isn't raining.

The contrapositive doesn't say anything different. It's just a commonsense rephrasing of the original statement. If you read that example too quickly, read it again. Do you see how the contrapositive just makes sense?

It's unnecessary—and often counterproductive—to worry about

contrapositives on the LSAT. Conditional statements are easier to grasp when you have an intuitive understanding of sufficient and necessary conditions.

Let's look at a real example.

Test 123, Section 3, Q22
If the price it pays for coffee beans continues to increase, the Coffee Shoppe will have to increase its prices. In that case, either the Coffee Shoppe will begin selling noncoffee products or its coffee sales will decrease. But selling noncoffee products will decrease the Coffee Shoppe's overall profitability. Moreover, the Coffee Shoppe can avoid a decrease in overall profitability only if its coffee sales do not decrease.

The question asks what must be true based on these facts.

If a student relies on diagrams and contrapositives, their work might look like this:

$$BPI \to SPI$$

$$SPI \to NC \text{ or } SD$$

$$NC \to PD$$

$$SD \to PD$$

$$BPI \to SPI \begin{subarray}{c} \nearrow NC \searrow \\ \text{or} \\ \searrow SD \nearrow \end{subarray} PD$$

$$\cancel{SPI} \to \cancel{BPI}$$

$$\cancel{NC} \text{ and } \cancel{SD} \to \cancel{SPI}$$

$$\cancel{PD} \to \cancel{NC}$$

$$\cancel{PD} \to \cancel{SD}$$

$$\cancel{PD} \begin{subarray}{c} \nearrow \cancel{NC} \searrow \\ \text{and} \\ \searrow \cancel{SD} \nearrow \end{subarray} \cancel{SPI} \to \cancel{BPI}$$

BPI = Bean Price Increases   NC = Non Coffee   PD = Profitability Decreases
SPI = Shop Prices Increase   SD = Sales Decrease

Chapter 11: Conditional Statements   77

Nathan

OMG, this diagram gives me flashbacks. I used to think that a whiteboard was critical infrastructure for teaching LSAT classes. How wrong we were, eh Ben? We were both casualties of our own previous encounters with legacy LSAT prep nonsense.

Ben

Yes, I failed to realize that as soon as you start diagramming, you stop thinking about the underlying, intuitive meaning of the original sentences. If you do the opposite—if you stop diagramming and start thinking about what the sentences are truly saying—it's shocking how much easier everything gets. It doesn't have to be as hard as we made it.

This setup is overcomplicated and time-consuming. The quickest way to the correct answer is to ditch the diagramming and understand the passage in commonsense terms:

> If bean prices keep going up, then the shop's prices will also go up.
> If the shop's prices go up, then they've either got to start selling noncoffee products or their coffee sales will go down.
> Either one of those things will result in decreased profitability.

What does all this mean for the coffee shop? Think about it. Don't expect the answer choices to help you figure it out.

If you were the shop owner, what would you want? You'd probably want the bean prices to stop going up—otherwise, you're losing profits.

Once you've simplified the passage in your own words, you don't need to worry about "contrapositives" to figure out the answer. And if you can't figure it out, it's doubtful that a diagram is going to help. It's certain that a diagram will take a bunch of time, and it's likely to make you more confused than you already were.

With just our commonsense understanding, let's look at the answer choices. Which one has to be true, given what we know?

> A. If the Coffee Shoppe's overall profitability decreases, the price it pays for coffee beans will have continued to increase.

This doesn't have to be true. If bean prices keep going up, then we know this place will lose money. But if they just lose money, we might not know why. It could be that bean prices kept going up. But it could also be a spike in rent, a recent lawsuit from an angry customer, or even Covid 2.0. The point: It said they'd lose money if bean prices keep going up. But it never said that was the only way to lose money. Using terms you might see on the LSAT, an increase in the price of coffee beans is sufficient to guarantee a decrease in profitability. But that increase might not be necessary—profitability could decrease for a million other reasons.

> B. If the Coffee Shoppe's overall profitability decreases, either it will have begun selling noncoffee products or its coffee sales will have decreased.

This is wrong for the same reason as A. Although selling noncoffee products or declining coffee sales would be sufficient for—or guarantee—lower profits, neither one is necessary for lower profits. Other things could lower their profitability.

> C. The Coffee Shoppe's overall profitability will decrease if the price it pays for coffee beans continues to increase.

This is exactly what we predicted.

> D. The price it pays for coffee beans cannot decrease without the Coffee Shoppe's overall profitability also decreasing.

This is out because the passage doesn't mention anything about what happens if the price of beans decreases.

> E. Either the price it pays for coffee beans will continue to increase or the Coffee Shoppe's coffee sales will increase.

This is out because the passage doesn't mention anything about what happens if the price of beans doesn't continue to increase.

Common sense trumps gimmicky diagramming strategies every time.

Chapter 12
Closed Question Types

Chapter Overview

We can divide Logical Reasoning questions into two broad categories: "Open" and "Closed," short for "Open record" and "Closed record."

Questions that ask you to find the answer that's proven by the information in the passage—and that information alone—are "Closed" because you can't look outside the "record" or the passage.

The poster child for this broad family of questions is Must Be True. Let's start with an example question and explanation. There's a ton of theory on this question type in the Appendix. Theory gets dry and boring, so don't waste time on it unless you really want to dig deep. You can always just drill more LR questions in the Demon—every explanation is its own lesson on the Must Be True question type.

Must Be True

Test 135, Section 4, Q6

The calm, shallow waters of coastal estuaries are easily polluted by nutrient-rich sewage. When estuary waters become overnutrified as a result, algae proliferate. The abundant algae, in turn, sometimes provide a rich food source for microorganisms that are toxic to fish, thereby killing most of the fish in the estuary.

Which one of the following can be properly inferred from the information above?

- A. Fish in an estuary that has been polluted by sewage are generally more likely to die from pollution than are fish in an estuary that has been polluted in some other way.
- B. In estuary waters that contain abundant algae, microorganisms that are toxic to fish reproduce more quickly than other types of microorganisms.
- C. Nutrients and other components of sewage do not harm fish in coastal estuaries in any way other than through the resulting proliferation of toxic microorganisms.
- D. Algae will not proliferate in coastal estuaries that are not polluted by nutrient-rich sewage.
- E. Overnutrifying estuary waters by sewage can result in the death of most of the fish in the estuary.

Explanation

Must Be True questions are about picking the boring, obvious, conservatively stated answer that's proven true by the given facts. The wrong answers will be different or extra.

- A. Nope. The facts say that sewage can kill fish, but maybe poisoning by cyanide or radiation kills fish even faster.
- B. Nope. We know microorganisms toxic to fish do well when there are abundant algae, but maybe other organisms (including the algae itself) do even better.
- C. Nope. We know that sewage harms fish via the algae / toxic organisms channel, but maybe sewage also poisons fish directly.

D. No, this answer confuses sufficient for necessary. We know that sewage causes algae to proliferate, but maybe chemical fertilizers, kids peeing in the river, or plain old sunny weather also cause algae to bloom.

E. Yep. Sewage pollution causes algae, algae causes toxic organisms, and toxic organisms kill most of the fish. So sewage pollution can kill most of the fish. This is 100% proven by the facts, so this is the answer.

See how everything you needed to know in order to answer this question was in the passage? That's what Closed questions are all about. Every Closed question simply asks us to pick the answer that's proven, or at least supported by the passage. Must Be True questions are the gold standard of Closed question types because the right answer needs to be 100% proven by the passage. This means the right answer will either be stated in the passage or will be an accurate inference based on the facts in the passage.

Other Closed Questions

Below you'll find a list of the rest of the Closed question types. The rest of this chapter might feel like drinking from a fire hose, but if you approach each of these question types with the mindset that the right answer will be supported or proven by the record, you'll be on the right track. Appendix A contains a sample question, an explanation, and a deep dive for each of these question types. You can also use Smart Drilling on lsatdemon.com to get reps in on each question type.

SUPPORTED

Supported questions ask us to pick the answer choice that is most strongly supported by the facts. The correct answer doesn't have to be true, but it will often be proven. Wrong answers will contain information that isn't confirmed by the passage or that outright contradicts the passage.

CONCLUSION

Conclusion questions ask us to pick the answer that represents the conclusion of the argument. The conclusion is just what the author is trying to prove. This is a Closed question type because the right answer will be stated in the passage. It may not be stated in the same way, but the right answer will have the same meaning as the argument's conclusion.

REASONING

Reasoning questions ask us to pick the answer that describes what the author does in the argument. These Closed questions should be looked at with a Must Be True mindset. The right answer will accurately describe the argument. Wrong answers will either contradict the argument or contain extra information.

REASONING (ROLE)

Reasoning (Role) questions will provide a portion of the argument and ask what function it plays in the argument as a whole. Is it the conclusion? Is it a premise supporting the conclusion? Is it a concession made by the author? The right answer will accurately express the role of the quoted portion of the argument.

FLAW

These questions ask us to choose the answer that accurately states the issue with the author's argument. Flaw questions are Closed because the right answer will be completely proven by the passage. When attacking a flaw question, consider the following questions:

1. **Did the author do this?**

    The right answer will describe a flaw that happens in the argument. So, if an answer choice describes something that the author never did, it can't be the right answer.

2. **If they did, is it a problem?**

    If an answer choice passes test one it also has to pass test two. If the author actually did what the answer choice describes, it also has to be an issue in the argument. An answer choice could accurately describe what the author did, but if it doesn't describe something wrong with the argument, it can't be the right answer.

If you can answer both questions with "yes" for an answer choice, it's the right answer. All of the wrong answers will fail on at least one of these questions.

NECESSARY ASSUMPTION

A necessary assumption is just something that the author must agree with. These questions ask us to pick the answer choice that's proven by the passage.

The right answer will be something that, if the argument is true, also has to be true. Wrong answers will simply say something that isn't proven.

DISAGREE/AGREE

The passage of a Disagree/Agree question will contain two arguments by two separate authors. Disagree questions ask us to pick the answer choice that describes what the authors don't agree on. Note that the right answer will be the one that one author would agree with, and the other disagrees with. If both would agree or disagree with the answer choice, it's not the right answer. It's about the authors disagreeing with each other, not with the answer choice. Similarly, Agree questions ask us to pick the answer choice that both authors would agree or disagree with. Again, it's about whether the authors agree with each other, not with the answer choice.

PARALLEL (REASONING)

On Parallel (Reasoning) questions, the LSAT will provide an argument as the passage and five more arguments as answer choices. The right answer will use the same logic as the original passage. Wrong answers will use different reasoning. These are Closed questions because the original passage contains all of the information needed to answer the question.

PARALLEL (FLAW)

Parallel (Flaw) questions will also provide an argument in the passage and five more arguments in the answer choices. The big difference between these and Parallel (Reasoning) questions is that the given argument on a Parallel (Flaw) question will always be invalid. The right answer will contain an argument with the same flaw as the original argument.

Sample questions, explanations, and deep dives for every question type covered in this chapter can be found in Appendix A. If you want to learn more about Closed questions now, go ahead and check it out. You now know enough to be dangerous on Logical Reasoning. Start drilling!

Chapter 13
Open Question Types

Chapter Overview

"Open" questions ask you to use new information to strengthen or weaken an argument or to resolve an apparent conflict between facts.

We think Weaken questions are the best example to understand and approach Open questions. Plus, in our opinion, they're pretty fun. If you don't agree yet, you'll come around. The approach to the passage will be almost the same as a Closed question. The big difference is that the answer choices won't ask you what the record proves. Instead, they will ask you to supplement the record in some way. Let's jump right in with a sample question.

Weaken

Test 123, Section 2, Q5
Scientist: Earth's average annual temperature has increased by about 0.5 degrees Celsius over the last century. This warming is primarily the result of the buildup of minor gases in the atmosphere, blocking the outward flow of heat from the planet.

Which one of the following, if true, would count as evidence against the scientist's explanation of Earth's warming?

- A. Only some of the minor gases whose presence in the atmosphere allegedly resulted in the phenomenon described by the scientist were produced by industrial pollution.
- B. Most of the warming occurred before 1940, while most of the buildup of minor gases in the atmosphere occurred after 1940.
- C. Over the last century, Earth received slightly more solar radiation in certain years than it did in others.
- D. Volcanic dust and other particles in the atmosphere reflect much of the Sun's radiation back into space before it can reach Earth's surface.
- E. The accumulation of minor gases in the atmosphere has been greater over the last century than at any other time in Earth's history.

Explanation

This one feels a little different, huh? That's because the argument, for once, seems close to being reasonable—there's no glaring flaw. All we have here is a description of a phenomenon and then an explanation of that phenomenon. There aren't a lot of moving parts. Still, the argument is far from complete.

According to the scientist, it's a fact that the Earth's average annual temperature has increased by about 0.5 degrees Celsius over the last century. We can't argue with this part. But the scientist goes on to explain this fact with a claim about causality: The warming is primarily the result of the buildup of gases in the atmosphere, which blocks the outward flow of heat from the planet.

Uh-oh. That's a claim of causation.

The LSAT has a field day with cause-and-effect arguments—I've seen Logical Reasoning sections where almost half of the questions had something to do with cause and effect. Here, we are asked to identify "evidence against" the scientist's explanation. Before I look at the answer choices, I'm going to think about two main problems that commonly pop up with this type of reasoning:

1. Is it possible that the Effect actually caused the alleged Cause? An obvious example of this is "Rich people own Bentleys, so Bentley ownership causes one to be rich." Silly, right? That's obviously backward. Well, we need to see if that might be happening in the scientist's argument. Here, the Effect was global warming, and the purported cause was a buildup of greenhouse gases. So ask yourself: Is it possible that the scientist has it the wrong way around? What if the warming actually caused the buildup of the gases? If that were true, then wouldn't the scientist look silly for claiming that the gases caused the warming?

2. Is it possible that some other Cause actually caused both the purported Cause and Effect? An obvious example of this is "Smokers make a lot of new friends outside bars, and they also get a lot of cancer. So making a lot of new friends outside bars causes you to get cancer." Silly, right? Clearly, smoking is the underlying cause of both making friends outside bars AND getting cancer. There's no causal relationship between making friends and getting cancer. So ask yourself: Is it possible that the scientist is ignoring some other factor? We can get creative here. What if, I don't know, radiation from Uranus was causing both the temperature increase and the buildup of atmospheric gases? If that were true, then wouldn't the scientist look silly for claiming that the gases caused the warming? (I'm sure that "Uranus" is not going to appear in the correct answer. But something that introduces a new factor like this could be perfect.)

I don't think either of these predictions is guaranteed to be correct. But both of these types of answers appear over and over and over as correct answers on old LSATs, so we have to look out for them. Okay, here we go. Remember, we're looking for the answer choice that would make the scientist's argument look stupid:

A. This doesn't matter. The cause of the gases themselves really isn't in question here. They could have been caused by industrial pollution, automobiles, or cattle; who cares? If answer A were true, the scientist would say, "So what? The gases still caused global warming." We're looking for an answer choice that leaves the scientist no reasonable response... we want to shut them up for good.

B. Hmm. If this is true, then the scientist's purported Cause happened after the scientist's purported Effect. Hey scientist, I have a question for you: How can the gases have caused global warming if the global warming happened first? I like this answer, because the scientist really can't say anything in response. (Also, notice that it kinda fits with my first prediction, the possibility that the warming actually caused the gases, instead of the other way around.) This one is a keeper.

C. Huh? Who cares. If this were true, the scientist would say something like, "My argument had nothing to do with solar radiation, but I'm not surprised that solar radiation fluctuates slightly from year to year." This does nothing to change the relationship between a buildup of atmospheric gases and the resulting global warming." There's no way this can be the answer.

D. Again, I don't see how this is relevant. The scientist would say "I'm not surprised that volcanic dust reflects the Sun's radiation. This fact does nothing to change the relationship between a buildup of atmospheric gases and the resulting global warming."

E. This would actually strengthen the scientist's argument, but we were looking for a weakener. If this were true, the scientist would say "yes, yes... since the Earth has been warming over the past century, this fact confirms my hypothesis that a buildup of gases has been causing global warming."

The answer that most weakens the scientist's argument is B, so that's our answer.

Weaken questions are a great example of understanding the bigger picture of Open questions. The right answer won't be proven by the passage like in a Closed question. Rather, the right answer is evidence against the argument. It's something that, if it's true, would be bad for the author's conclusion.

Other Open Questions

Open questions will ask you to add information to the argument, or at least, evaluate possibilities outside of what is proven by the facts. For this reason, we think that Open questions can be pretty fun—you get to use your imagination! Importantly, the right answers will still be one hundred percent, conclusively correct and wrong answers will be demonstrably incorrect. Just like on Closed questions, your job is to find what's wrong in each wrong answer, and understand what's so good about the right answer. Let's take a quick look at the rest of the Open question types.

STRENGTHEN

Strengthen questions are the separated-at-birth twin of Weaken questions. Everything about them is the exact same, except instead of trying to hurt the author's conclusion, the right answer will help the author's conclusion. The right answer to a Strengthen question will often be either a Necessary Assumption or a Sufficient Assumption, as both of these question types ask us to strengthen the argument as well. However, the right answer can also be information that neither has to be true, nor completely fixes the argument. All we need on a Strengthen question is to move the needle slightly in the argument's favor.

SUFFICIENT ASSUMPTION

Sufficient Assumption questions ask you to pick the answer choice that, if true, would completely prove the argument's conclusion. Although the "assumption" in the name leads some students to believe this question type is similar to Necessary Assumption questions, the two are very different. The right answer to a Sufficient Assumption question doesn't have to be true according to the facts; rather, if it were true, it would make the argument valid.

PARADOX

Paradox questions ask you to explain or resolve an unexpected outcome. The argument will give a set of facts that would support a certain result, but instead, an unexpected result will be given. Your job is to fill in the gaps to explain how, if the facts in the passage are true, the unexpected result could have happened.

EVALUATE

Evaluate questions will present a flawed argument and give you the opportunity to ask the author a question. On Evaluate questions, the conclusion itself may or may not be true, but the evidence won't guarantee that it is. The correct answer will contain a question that, if the author were to answer it, would provide the most useful information in evaluating whether the conclusion is true or not.

START PRACTICING

That's all of the Open question types. If you want to keep digging, you can go to lsatdemon.com and drill right now, or you can go to Appendix B for sample questions and deep dives on each question type discussed in this chapter.

Chapter 14
Word Strength

Chapter Overview

Lawyers are gladiators of the English language. The best lawyers have fantastic control over the words they use. The LSAT frequently tests your knowledge of what specific words mean in ways that you don't even notice. Luckily, we're going to tell you all about it. In this chapter, we'll explain why some words are absolute in their meaning and others are subjective or relative.

Some, Most, and All

Some words are stronger than others. They say more.

Consider the words "some" and "most." If I told you that "some Americans hate Halo Top ice cream," you'd know that a few Americans hated that so-called dessert. But you wouldn't know how many. You'd know that at least one American hated it, but that's it. Maybe 100 hate it, or maybe 900, or maybe more than 300 million. You'd have no clue. But if I told you that "most Americans hate Halo Top," you'd know that more than half of them hated it. Given that there are roughly 340 million Americans, at least 170 million people must hate Halo Top. That one small shift in wording makes a big difference in meaning. In short, "most" is stronger than "some."

Not surprisingly, "all" is stronger than "most." If I told you that "all Americans hate Halo Top," you'd know that every single American hated Halo Top. It wouldn't matter where they were in the world, how old they were, how annoying they were, or what they ate for breakfast. If they were an American, you'd know that they hated it. "All" is stronger than "most," and "most" is stronger than "some." And if you're curious, "no" is just as strong as "all." It's just negative.

Now let's assume there are 100 waiters in the world, none of whom serve Halo Top, thankfully. Here's how many waiters could be rich under each scenario:

- Some waiters are rich means "at least one waiter is rich." (1–100)
- Most waiters are rich means "more than half of the waiters are rich." (51–100)
- All waiters are rich means "every waiter is rich." (100)
- No waiters are rich means "every waiter is not rich." (0)
- Not all waiters are rich means "at least one waiter is not rich." (0–99)

Why does this matter? The LSAT tests your knowledge of word strength frequently. The good news is that word strength is easy. Everything we just told you is common sense. Maybe you've never thought of it this way, but you instinctively know what some, most, and all mean. And if you didn't know before, you do now.

Subjective Terms

The test-writers, of course, don't always use "some," "most," or "all" to express their point. They might use "many," "majority," "often," or something else.

So it's important to learn what words mean. Is "many" stronger than "most," for instance? Or are they just as strong as each other? It turns out that "many" is weaker than "most" because it's subjective. It means the same thing as "some"—at least one. If you walked into a Honda dealer, for example, and asked the sales manager how long the transmission should last on a brand-new Honda Civic, he might tell you "many years." If you don't press him on his answer, you two might walk away thinking very different things. You might think he meant about ten years, while he really just meant about five years.

That's because the word "many" is subjective. It depends on what the speaker thinks "many" means in that situation. Granted, it has to be more than zero. So the sales manager must have meant "at least a year." But we don't know more than that. The best way to learn what words mean "some," what words mean "most," and what words mean "all" is just to try and fail.

In the next section, you'll see several words. For each one, decide whether it means "some" (because it's subjective), "most" (because it means more than half), or "all" (because it means every single one).

Subjective terms quiz

Which word—"some," "most," or "all"—most closely matches the meaning of each phrase?

1. almost all
2. any
3. certain
4. each
5. every
6. few
7. frequently
8. generally
9. likely
10. majority
11. many
12. nearly all
13. numerous
14. often
15. probably
16. rarely
17. several
18. sometimes
19. tends to
20. there are
21. typically
22. usually

Answers

1. most
2. all
3. some
4. all
5. all
6. some
7. some
8. most
9. most
10. most
11. some
12. most
13. some
14. some
15. most
16. some
17. some
18. some
19. most
20. some
21. most
22. most

Word Strength

Words used to quantify something fall into these three categories: *some, most,* and *all.*

Words that mean *some* are weaker than words that mean *most.* And words that mean *most* are weaker than words that mean *all.*

Some	Most	All
1-100	51-100	100
Some Few Rarely Certain There are Sometimes Many Several Numerous Frequently Often	Most Almost Majority Nearly all Generally Tends to Typically Usually Likely Probably	All Any Each Every
Weaker	Stronger	Strongest

Words also become stronger as the quantities they indicate become more specific (not larger). We can use this same reasoning to account for negative terms: "No" is just as strong as "all" because they are equally specific. A "minority" is just as strong as a "majority" or "most" because they are equally specific. "Not all" is just as strong as "some" because they are equally specific.

To be clear, words that mean "some" don't all have the exact same meaning. If you use the words "some" and "many" in the same sentence, for example, they don't mean the same thing, even though both mean "at least one." Context matters.

Relative vs. Absolute Terms

If a word or phrase compares something to something else, then it's relative. Otherwise, it's absolute. I can say that you're "tall" without referring to anyone else. You're just tall. So that's absolute.

But when I say that you're "taller than Joe" or "the tallest person in school," I have to compare you to at least one other person. So "taller" and "tallest" are relative terms because you're only taller or the tallest relative to other people.

Logically, you can't jump from a relative term to an absolute one or vice versa.

Even if you're the "tallest" person in the room, for instance, that doesn't necessarily mean that you're "tall." You might be in a room full of small children. Similarly, if you're the "poorest" managing partner at Skadden, then you might not be "poor." You're just "poorer" than all the other managing partners at Skadden. Bummer.

Similarly, in a Parallel Reasoning question, if the original argument has a premise that's relative, then the correct answer will likely have a premise that's relative as well. In other words, switching to an absolute term wouldn't be logical or parallel.

Examples

Absolute	Relative	Relative
Tall	Taller	Tallest
Good	Better	Best
Common	More common	Most common
Likely	More likely	Most likely

Chapter 15
Types of Claims

Chapter Overview

On your journey to LSAT mastery, you will read a lot of claims. Not all are created equal.

In this chapter, we'll unpack all you need to know about claims. Remember, the LSAT is easy, and claims are, too. You've known most of this stuff since you were a kid. But since it's mostly common sense, you probably haven't formalized your knowledge of different types of claims. That's what we'll do in this chapter. Don't overcomplicate it.

Facts

"Facts" are information the author treats as true.

These facts tell us that the world is getting warmer:

- The world is getting warmer.
- It has been conclusively proven that the world is getting warmer.
- Scientists correctly believe that the world is getting warmer.

And these facts tell us that the world isn't getting warmer:

- The world is not getting warmer.
- The belief that the world is getting warmer is false.
- Scientists incorrectly believe that the world is getting warmer.

The truth of these statements in the real world doesn't matter. What matters is that the author believes they're true.

Beliefs

"Beliefs" reveal what others believe.

When someone tells us what other people believe, we know what those people believe, but we have no idea whether their belief is true:

- Scientists believe that the world is getting warmer.
- Scientists argue that the world is getting warmer.
- Scientists assert that the world is getting warmer.
- Scientists claim that the world is getting warmer.

For all we know, the world is getting colder—or staying the same. It doesn't matter that we know what scientists think or say. Even scientists can be wrong.

To be clear, we're pretty sure that they're right. But the LSAT doesn't care what we think. All that matters are the words on the page.

Studies

The next claims are tougher, but they're common sense. The authors probably believe that the world is getting warmer. But we still don't know for sure. Studies can show something and be wrong:

- Studies show that the world is getting warmer.
- Research suggests that the world is getting warmer.

Treat studies as evidence. The examples above give us reason to believe that the world is getting warmer, but they don't prove that the world is getting warmer. The only thing that studies actually prove on the LSAT is that there was a study with a particular result.

Normative vs. Descriptive Claims

A normative claim tells you how the world should be, while a descriptive claim tells you how it is. You can't logically jump from one to the other. Take a look at the following example:

James should pay his taxes. Therefore, James will pay his taxes.

This definitely doesn't have to be true. Most of us should work out more, but that doesn't mean we will. When an argument switches from a normative claim about how things should be to a descriptive claim about how things are, jump all over it. That's a logical no-go and a common flaw on the LSAT.

CAN VS. WILL

Although "can" and "will" claims are descriptive, you also can't jump from one to the other. Just because Joe can eat pancakes doesn't mean that he will. That said, if he can't eat pancakes, then we know that he won't.

By the way, are you doubting that last inference? "Wait," you say, "maybe he can't eat pancakes because he's allergic to gluten, but he does so anyway by accident. Ha, so even if someone can't do something, they still might do it."

Sorry, but if someone is allergic to gluten, it's not true that they can't eat pancakes. They can, but they shouldn't because they might have a reaction and even die. Technically speaking, though, they can still eat pancakes. The LSAT requires you to read every word literally. When a premise on the LSAT tells you that something can't happen, it cannot happen. So if a premise says, "Nathan can't eat pancakes," then Nathan is somehow physically unable to eat pancakes. However, if a conclusion tells you that something can't happen, it's fair game. Go on attack mode.

Should	Can	Will
Normative	Descriptive	Descriptive
Should Ought	Can Able Ability Possible	Will Did Do And a bunch more... Buy Sell Eat Sleep Gallop Run Fly Cry Yell Invent And so on...

Now it's your turn. Read the arguments below. After each claim, take a second to identify whether it's a fact, a belief, or a study and if it's normative or descriptive. Once you're done, check the answer key at the bottom of the page.

Test 135, Section 1, Q13

(1) Researchers have studied the cost-effectiveness of growing halophytes—salt-tolerant plant species—for animal forage. (2) Halophytes require more water than conventional crops, but can be irrigated with seawater, and pumping seawater into farms near sea level is much cheaper than pumping freshwater from deep wells. (3) Thus, seawater agriculture near sea level should be cost-effective in desert regions (4) although its yields are smaller than traditional, freshwater agriculture.

Test 135, Section 4, Q23

Biologist: (5) Researchers believe that dogs are the descendants of domesticated wolves that were bred to be better companions for humans. (6) It has recently been found that some breeds of dog are much more closely related genetically to wolves than to most other breeds of dog. (7) This shows that some dogs are descended from wolves that were domesticated much more recently than others.

Answers

1. Fact (descriptive). The author doesn't give us the results of the study, they just tell us that it happened. Thus, they treat the fact that a study happened as true.
2. Fact (descriptive)
3. Fact (normative)
4. Fact (descriptive)
5. Belief (descriptive)
6. Study (descriptive)
7. Fact (descriptive)

Chapter 16
Most Common Flaws

Chapter Overview

One reason we can confidently say the LSAT is easy is because it repeats itself constantly. In this chapter, we'll talk about some of the most common flaws that appear in LR.

Sufficient vs. Necessary

Many people think about if-clauses incorrectly. Consider this stupid rule:

If you eat at Chipotle, then you will get a special tax credit.

What do you need to do to get that "special tax credit"?

If your gut reaction is "eat at Chipotle," you're not alone, but you're misinterpreting the word "need." Eating at Chipotle is a sufficient condition. In other words, eating there guarantees that you'll get the special tax credit.

But is that the only way to get the credit?

We have no idea. We haven't been given any other information. So although eating at Chipotle might be the only way to get the credit, there could be other ways. Maybe you can get the credit by eating at McDonald's or by just calling 911. Given what little was said here, there's no way to know. All we know is that eating at Chipotle is one way of getting the credit. Yet notice what we asked:

What do you need to do to get that credit?

The short answer is that we don't know. The rule doesn't tell us what is "necessary" for the tax credit; it tells us only what is "sufficient" for that credit. Eating at Chipotle is sufficient for getting the tax credit, and getting the tax credit is necessary for eating at Chipotle. But the reverse is not necessarily true. Eating at Chipotle might not be "necessary" for getting the credit. You might be able to get the credit some other way.

In other words, if you initially answered "eat at Chipotle," your mind turned that sufficient condition into a necessary condition. So watch out.

The LSAT also tests the opposite version of this flaw, confusing a necessary condition for a sufficient condition. Keeping the above example about Chipotle and tax credits, what would you say if we made the following conclusion?

"Amanda got a special tax credit, so Amanda must have eaten Chipotle."

Hopefully you see that this doesn't have to be true given the rule provided. We know that eating Chipotle is enough to guarantee the tax credit, however, we don't know that it's the only way to receive the tax credit. What if there are other ways to get the tax credit, and Amanda did one of those? The necessary condition can occur independently from the sufficient condition. Don't let the LSAT trick you by confusing necessary and sufficient!

This question confuses sufficient and necessary conditions. Give it a try!

Test 141, Section 4, Q25
Roberta is irritable only when she is tired, and loses things only when she is tired. Since she has been yawning all day, and has just lost her keys, she is almost certainly irritable.

The reasoning above is flawed in that it

A. Infers from a correlation between tiredness and yawning that tiredness causes yawning

B. Assumes the conclusion that it sets out to prove

C. Generalizes on the basis of a single instance

D. Takes a necessary condition for Roberta's losing things to be a sufficient condition

E. Takes a necessary condition for Roberta's being irritable to be a sufficient condition

Explanation

The first clause of the passage is easy. If Roberta is irritable, she must be tired. If she loses things, she must be tired. Ok, so we have two sufficient conditions for Roberta being tired.

My guess is that the conclusion will spin these conditions around and try to justify something we do not know to be true. And it does. Assuming yawning is a good indicator of tiredness (this is me helping the argument, it should have stated that) and that Roberta has just lost something, can we conclude she is irritable? No way. The argument takes a necessary condition of being irritable (Roberta is tired) to be a sufficient one. The argument flips the first clause around to say, "If Roberta is tired, then she is irritable," when it was exactly the opposite.

This is a Flaw question. I know exactly what the flaw is, and I'm excited to disrespect these wrong answers. I took a little extra time to think about the passage and find my objection to make quick work of these wrong answers.

- A. I stopped after correlation. There's no "correlation/causation" flaw here.
- B. Nope. This is a very common wrong answer on Flaw questions. B is quite literally saying the author said the same exact things in the evidence as she did in the conclusion. That's the opposite of what's really happening.
- C. Nope. The evidence is actually quite general. This is not our sufficient/necessary flaw anyway. Next.
- D. We're getting warmer, but this is still wrong. The author's conclusion is not about losing things. It's trying to prove Roberta will be irritable. This is not accurately characterizing the conclusion or the flaw. Just because the words "sufficient" and "necessary" appear in the answer does not mean it matches our prediction.
- E. Yes, this is our answer. This answer accurately characterizes the flaw and the conclusion. The author is trying to prove Roberta will be irritable by making it a necessary condition of tiredness. But irritability was the sufficient condition in the evidence. You cannot switch the two around from the evidence to the conclusion. That violates the most basic LSAT rule.

Correlation vs. Causation

While correlation may be evidence of causation, correlation alone does not prove causation.

In these arguments, the author tells you that two things are correlated and then mistakenly concludes that one of those things must cause the other.

CORRELATION

The author might tell you, for example, that people who buy an Apple iPhone are more likely to buy Bose headphones than other people.

That's a correlation because there's a relationship between buying an iPhone and buying Bose headphones. But we don't know why they're correlated.

CAUSATION

Does buying an Apple iPhone make people want to buy Bose headphones? Or does buying Bose headphones make people want to buy an Apple iPhone? Or does something else, such as having a bunch of money, make people want to buy both?

Even though we don't know for sure, the author will often go on to conclude that buying or owning an Apple iPhone entices people to buy Bose headphones. That could be true, but we don't know for sure. That's a flaw because conclusions need to be proven—not just supported.

In short, the author jumps from a premise showing us that two things are correlated to a conclusion asserting that one of those things causes the other.

CORRELATIVE VS. CAUSAL STATEMENTS

To figure out whether a sentence is asserting correlation or causation, focus on the **verb** of the sentence:

Is it saying that the first thing **affects** the second thing? *If so, that's causation.*

Or is it saying that the first thing **is**, **has**, or **does** the second thing? *If so, that's correlation.*

These sentences are causal because they say that one thing affects the other:

- Sodium not used by the body **will increase** blood pressure.

- His behavior sometimes **leads to** an overall poor performance in his job.
- Situational factors **account for** most code-switching.
- Facebook is a **factor** in shaping the social morals of modern America.
- These vegetables were depleted of nutrients **because of** an earlier failure to rotate crops.

These sentences are only correlative because they say only that these two things happen together. We still don't know why.

- Democracies **are** more likely than nondemocratic forms of government to **have** policymakers who understand the complexity of governmental issues.
- Those who buy expensive running shoes **tend** to exercise more often than those who buy cheap ones.

TYPICAL ARGUMENT

It's wrong, as the LSAT puts it, to "conclude causation from mere correlation":

Premise: People with A are more likely to have B.

Conclusion: Therefore, A causes B.

That could be true. But there are at least two other possibilities:

- Maybe B causes A, or
- Maybe C causes both A and B

For that reason, the conclusion that A causes B has not been proven.

This question confuses correlation and causation. See if you can catch it in the argument.

Test 141, Section 4, Q3

Moore: Sunscreen lotions, which are designed to block skin-cancer-causing ultraviolet radiation, do not do so effectively. Many scientific studies have shown that people who have consistently used these lotions develop, on average, as many skin cancers as those who have rarely, if ever, used them.

The reasoning in Moore's argument is most vulnerable to criticism on the grounds that the argument

- A. Takes for granted that there are no other possible health benefits of using sunscreen lotions other than blocking skin-cancer-causing ultraviolet radiation
- B. Fails to distinguish between the relative number of cases of skin cancer and the severity of those cases in measuring effectiveness at skin cancer prevention
- C. Fails to consider the effectiveness of sunscreen lotions that are not specifically designed to block skin-cancer-causing ultraviolet radiation
- D. Relies on evidence regarding the probability of people in different groups developing cancer that, in principle, would be impossible to challenge
- E. Overlooks the possibility that people who consistently use sunscreen lotions spend more time in the sun, on average, than people who do not

Explanation

The argument basically says, "There's no correlation, therefore there's no causation." It cites evidence that people who do use sunscreens have just as many skin cancers as people who don't (in other words, there's no negative correlation between sunscreen use and skin cancers). The argument then leaps to the conclusion that sunscreen doesn't prevent skin cancers.

This argument is exactly like saying, "There are more police in high-crime areas, therefore police don't prevent crime" or "There are just as many overweight people in the gym as there are in normal life, therefore the gym doesn't help people maintain their weight."

Flaw questions ask us to find the answer that accurately describes what the argument did wrong.

A. Nope. The argument doesn't do this. Sunscreen might prevent diabetes for all we know—the argument is only about whether sunscreen prevents cancer. Other diseases are irrelevant.

B. This is wrong because even though the argument did fail to discuss the severity of the cases, we don't know whether they would be the same, better, or worse for people who use sunscreen. So it's not clear how this information would affect the argument. It could help it.

C. No. Dumb. The argument is only about sunscreen lotions that are specifically designed to block skin-cancer-causing ultraviolet radiation. Other sunscreen lotions are irrelevant.

D. Huh? We have no justification for this accusation. Why would it be "impossible to challenge" the evidence about skin cancers in sunscreen users vs. non-users? If we pick this answer, we're just making stuff up. We have no idea where the evidence came from. We could ask. We don't get to leap to "your evidence is impossible to challenge."

E. Yes. I'm a golfer, so I spend a lot of time in the sun. I wear sunscreen (most of the time) when I play golf. I am almost certain to get skin cancer at some point in my life because I spend so much time in the sun. If I didn't wear sunscreen, I'd be even more likely to get skin cancer. Sunscreen reduces my risk, but it doesn't reduce it to zero. People who never go in the sun don't need sunscreen. But their risk isn't zero either.

Part vs. Whole

"Part-to-whole" reasoning makes the mistake of assuming individual traits apply to a group. Consider the following example:

Every employee of Enron was a person. Therefore Enron was a person.

Nope. The whole does not always have a characteristic that each individual part has. Like how all of Enron's employees being people doesn't make Enron a person.

"Whole-to-part" reasoning does the inverse, assuming that a group trait applies to an individual member. Here's an example:

The population of Palo Alto is extraordinarily wealthy. Samantha lives in Palo Alto, so Samantha is extraordinarily wealthy.

While the average income in Palo Alto might be high, that doesn't mean that Samantha herself is rolling in it. Maybe she's a broke college student living with six roommates.

Characteristics of individual components don't always apply to the whole. Similarly, properties of the whole don't necessarily apply to each of its components. Look for the part vs. whole flaw in the following question.

Test D, Section 4, Q6
Each member of the rock band Velvet Chaos is a talented musician who has achieved impressive commercial success in their own right. So Velvet Chaos is undoubtedly going to be a hit.

The argument above is most vulnerable to criticism on the grounds that it

- A. Assumes that talent in one domain guarantees the same level of success in a different context
- B. Confuses a necessary condition for achieving commercial success with a sufficient condition for achieving commercial success
- C. Illicitly shifts the meaning of success in its conclusion
- D. Takes for granted that the qualities and achievements of individual members will translate into success for the group as a whole
- E. Presumes, without justification, that individual talent is the only thing required for commercial success

Explanation
Some supergroups do well. Others get mixed reviews. No offense to fans of Super Heavy, but is anyone surprised that Mick Jagger meets Reggae meets Bollywood didn't go the distance?

This argument is a textbook example of the part-to-whole flaw. The fact that each member of the band is talented and successful doesn't mean the band will be successful. They could flop for any number of reasons. We're looking for an answer choice that calls out the erroneous part-to-whole assumption.

- A. The argument doesn't assume that individual talent alone is enough to make the band a hit. It says that talent and previous success together are enough.

B. There's no conditional reasoning in this argument, so this is out.

C. The argument is consistent in its reference to success. It talks about individual commercial success, then being a "hit." Those mean the same thing.

D. The argument takes a characteristic of each part of the band and applies it to the whole. Individual traits, such as talent and commercial success, don't automatically extend to the group. For instance, every employee of a corporation is a person, but corporations themselves are not people. This is the right answer.

E. Like answer A, this one ignores each member's individual success. The argument assumes that both individual talent and individual success—not just talent—are enough to guarantee success, not required for individual success.

Bad Samples

Arguments often rely on empirical evidence for their factual basis. Strong evidence requires valid methodology, including the use of representative samples.

Let's say you want to figure out the average lifespan of all human beings. A representative sample of such a broad population would need to reflect the vast diversity of the human population. Attributes like gender, race, socioeconomic status, culture, health, ability status, and lifestyle should all be represented.

If a sample is not representative, then observations drawn from it are not generalizable to the broader population.

COMMON BAD SAMPLES

Nonrandom samples: If you're trying to conclude something about human beings in general, but your sample is composed entirely of Portuguese men, then your sample is biased. It fails to represent the racial and gender variations that exist across all human beings.

Insufficient sample size: The smaller the sample size, the less likely it is to accurately reflect the diversity of the broader population. For example, you can't claim that all humans can live to the age of 105 merely because your great-uncle just turned 105 years old—he's an outlier.

IDENTIFYING BAD SAMPLES

If the passage only mentions the results and doesn't mention the samples that were used, there's no reason to suspect a bad sample. But if the passage mentions a sample and there's a clear reason it might be biased or unrepresentative, sampling flaws are fair game.

On Weaken questions, it's much easier to pick an answer about sample sizes because the burden is on the answer choice to prove the sample was bad. On Flaw questions, in contrast, the answer choice must start with "fails to consider the possibility that" unless there's a sampling issue evident in the passage itself.

This practice question has a bad sample flaw. Let's see if you can solve it!

Test 141, Section 2, Q3
Some video game makers have sold the movie rights for popular games. However, this move is rarely good from a business perspective. After all, StarQuanta sold the movie rights to its popular game Nostrama, but the poorly made film adaptation of the game was hated by critics and the public alike. Subsequent versions of the Nostrama video game, although better than the original, sold poorly.

The reasoning in the argument is most vulnerable to criticism in that the argument:

A. Draws a general conclusion on the basis of just one individual case

B. Infers that a product will be disliked by the public merely from the claim that the product was disliked by critics

C. Restates as a conclusion a claim earlier presented as evidence for that conclusion

D. Takes for granted that products with similar content that are in different media will be of roughly equal popularity

E. Treats a requirement for a product to be popular as something that ensures that a product will be popular

Explanation

I predicted the answer here. The argument took one anecdotal case—the tragic case of the garbage video game movie Nostrama—and leaped to an overly broad conclusion about video game movies generally. The LSAT tests this flaw fairly regularly, so I predicted that "small sample/overgeneralization" would be the answer. And sure enough, it was.

A. Yep, exactly. I'm no statistician, but I know that a sample size of one isn't enough to prove a trend.

B. The argument didn't do this. The argument says both the critics and the public hated the film. It didn't say "critics hated it, so the public will too."

C. Nah, there's no circular reasoning here. This would be the answer if it had gone "you shouldn't make movies out of video games because it is a bad idea to take a video game and make a movie out of it." That's not what they did here—they cited evidence about what happened with Nostrama.

D. The argument actually did the opposite of this. Nostrama was popular as a video game, but a complete flop in the different medium of film. The argument doesn't assume that anything that's popular in one form will be equally popular in others.

E. No way; the argument didn't confuse sufficient and necessary.

The correct answer is A because it correctly describes a common (and predictable) LSAT flaw.

Disconnect

A common logical flaw is a simple disconnect between the premises and the conclusion. This manifests in a couple of ways:

1. The conclusion introduces a new idea.

Take this argument, for example:

> Dogs that have fleas scratch a lot. Dogs that scratch a lot are annoying. Thus, dogs that have fleas are bad dogs.

Where did "bad dogs" come from? There's nothing in the premises about what makes dogs bad. This creates a disconnect between the premises and the conclusion. Just because a dog is annoying doesn't mean that dog is bad. Without evidence stating what makes a dog bad, the conclusion cannot include bad dogs.

2. **The conclusion goes too far with ideas discussed in the argument.**

This occurs when the argument turns up the heat a bit too much, creating a disconnect between the premises and the conclusion. It makes a conclusion based on insufficient evidence.

Take this argument, for example:

> If John goes out today, he'll go to the grocery store or hardware store, but not both. John went out today, so he must have gone to the grocery store.

Going to the grocery store is certainly a possibility for John. But the argument cannot conclude, based solely on the fact that he went out, that he went to the grocery store. That's a conclusion based on insufficient evidence. Why couldn't he have gone to the hardware store instead? See the disconnect?

Stay attuned to this flaw. It's tested often on the LSAT.

See if you can spot the disconnect in this question.

Test 135, Section 2, Q19
One theory to explain the sudden extinction of all dinosaurs points to "drug overdoses" as the cause. Angiosperms, a certain class of plants, first appeared at the time that dinosaurs became extinct. These plants produce amino-acid-based alkaloids that are psychoactive agents. Most plant-eating mammals avoid these potentially lethal poisons because they taste bitter. Moreover, mammals have livers that help detoxify such drugs. However, dinosaurs could neither taste the bitterness nor detoxify the substance once it was ingested. This theory receives its strongest support from the fact that it helps explain why so many dinosaur fossils are found in unusual and contorted positions.

Which one of the following, if true, would most undermine the theory presented above?

A. Many fossils of large mammals are found in contorted positions.
B. Angiosperms provide a great deal of nutrition.
C. Carnivorous dinosaurs mostly ate other, vegetarian, dinosaurs that fed on angiosperms

- D. Some poisonous plants do not produce amino-acid-based alkaloids.
- E. Mammals sometimes die of drug overdoses from eating angiosperms.

Explanation

Have you ever heard the phrase, "It's so wrong that it's right?" That doesn't apply here. This argument is so wrong that it's just really, really wrong. "Fossils are found in unusual and contorted positions. Therefore, dinosaurs must have been tripping on magic mushrooms?" Are you kidding me?

We're asked to undermine this theory, which should be fairly easy, given that it's the stupidest thing that I've ever read. There are about a zillion reasons why fossils could be found in contorted positions that make more sense than tripping on drugs. Geological forces, for one thing, would have had millions of years to contort the fossils after the dinosaurs were already dead. Or how about a T-Rex ripping the head off a Brontosaurus while eating him, thus leaving the loser's body a contorted mess? Sure, the author gave us some evidence, but there's a massive disconnect between what the author thinks the evidence proves and what the evidence actually proves. This argument is comically bad.

- A. This weakens the theory, because unless whales and elephants were also tripping on mushrooms then it provides a disconnect between "found in contorted positions" and "tripping." This takes the disconnect that was already there and widens it.
- B. How is nutrition relevant? The nutjob would say, "Yes, I know that magic mushrooms are nutritious! And they also made the dinosaurs see purple unicorns."
- C. I don't see how carnivores vs. herbivores is relevant, either. The nutjob might say, "Even if the herbivores were the only ones eating the mushrooms, the carnivores were also tripping off the herbivore carcasses."
- D. Nah. This answer is very weak because of the word "some." "Some" just means "one or more," and I don't see how "one or more poisonous plants do not produce alkaloids" would ruin the idea that the dinosaurs were tripping.
- E. This would only strengthen the argument, not weaken it.

Our answer is A, because it comes the closest to saying, "There are a lot of other reasons a fossil might be found in contorted positions besides tripping." This might be the strangest LSAT question of all time, by the way.

Chapter 17
Closed Question Types (RC)

Chapter Overview

Just like in Logical Reasoning, questions in Reading Comprehension can be broken down into two categories: Open and Closed. On all Closed questions, the right answer will be completely proven by the passage.

Let's jump into the poster child of Closed Reading Comprehension questions: Main Point.

Main Point

Main Point questions ask you to choose the answer that best describes the message the author of the passage is trying to get across. In a way, this makes Main Point questions similar to Conclusion questions in Logical Reasoning. As you read, you should regularly ask yourself, "Why does this document exist?" and "What does the author want me to know?" The answer to these two questions will be the main point of the passage.

Below, you'll find a step-by-step guide to solving Main Point questions. If you want to practice, jump over to lsatdemon.com where you can drill RC passages for free. Every question is accompanied by written and video explanations for you to deepen your understanding.

Prediction
- Restate the main point in your head before reading the answers.
- If you need to do so, scan back over the passage to see the big picture.

Answer choices
As you read each answer, ask yourself:

- Does this answer match my prediction?

Wrong answers are usually inaccurate or too narrow. An inaccurate answer will often contradict something that was said in the passage or introduce a new idea that was never discussed. An answer that's too narrow will often restate one of the author's premises but not the main point.

When debating two unattractive answers, an incomplete answer is better than an inaccurate one. On the LSAT, inaccuracy is the greatest sin. A complete answer is better than an incomplete one. But incomplete answers can be correct, while inaccurate ones are always wrong.

Other Closed Types

SUPPORTED

Supported questions ask you to pick the answer that is most in alignment with the passage. The key here is that the right answer doesn't have to be completely proven (although it may be), but it absolutely cannot contradict the passage in any way. You can think of Supported questions as Must Be Trues with a little bit of wiggle room. With a solid grasp of the passage, the right answers should jump off the page.

STATED

The task on these questions is straightforward: What did the passage actually say? The correct answer doesn't have to be directly or explicitly stated, but all the information in the correct answer will be found in the passage. Wrong answers will either contradict the passage or include information that isn't proven.

AGREE

These questions pick a "character" from the passage, whether it's the author or a specific person the author wrote about, and ask which answer choice that "character" is most likely to agree with. The correct answer will be proven by the passage, and the wrong answers won't. Agree questions often ask about the author's opinion, so pay attention when the author signals how they feel about what they're saying, whether explicitly or implicitly.

MEANING

Meaning questions pull a specific word or phrase from the passage and ask you to choose the answer that best represents that word's meaning. While a strong vocabulary will help answer these questions, the words chosen are often obscure. So you will need to rely on context.

TONE

Tone questions ask you to choose the answer that best describes the author's attitude about something they wrote. Sometimes the author will outright praise, agree with, or disagree with what they write, other times they will only cue you in with subtle signs such as positive or negative adverbs, implicit agreement, or sarcasm.

PURPOSE

Purpose questions isolate a part of the passage and ask you why it was included in the broader passage. These questions are very similar to Role questions in Logical Reasoning. Is the selected text part of the author's main point? Is it support for their main point? Is it an example, a theory, or something else? As with all Closed questions, the correct answer will be proven by the passage, and the wrong answers will include some type of inaccuracy.

ORGANIZATION

Organization questions ask you to take a 40,000-foot view of the passage and determine how it's organized. To answer these questions, identify what the main point is and why the author believes it. From there, it should be simple to explain how the passage arrives at that main point. The correct answer can feel slightly incomplete, but it absolutely cannot be inaccurate in any way.

ANALOGY

Analogy questions point to a situation or example in the passage and give five more situations or examples in the answers. The correct answer will be the one that is most analogous to the situation cited in the passage. As with all Closed questions, the correct answer will be proven by the passage—in other words, the relevant situation or example in the passage will mirror the correct answer.

Chapter 18
Open Question Types (RC)

Chapter Overview

You just learned about Closed questions on RC, which make up the vast majority of the questions you'll see. However, from time to time, the LSAT will throw Open questions into an RC section. No need to panic, Open questions on RC are easy, too.

On RC, there are only two Open question types: Strengthen and Weaken. These questions function nearly identically to their Logical Reasoning counterparts. The author of the passage tries to prove something but stumbles. Your job is either to help them or to show them why they could be wrong.

> **Ben**
> Open RC questions are a great example of how the skills you learn in LR transfer to RC and vice versa. While arguments are most commonly associated with Logical Reasoning, Reading Comprehension contains plenty. RC passages try to either inform you or persuade you. Open questions on RC will relate to some sort of argument within the passage, so you can apply many of the skills you've already learned from Open LR questions.

Nathan

Good arguments are rare in real life and rarer yet on the LSAT. So assuming you're looking at a bad argument, it's possible to either strengthen or weaken that argument by adding new information. That's what Open questions in RC ask you to do.

Strengthen

For Strengthen questions, all you need to do is understand what the passage says, predict what the correct answer should look like, and eliminate wrong answers based on your prediction.

Prediction
- Go back to the passage to figure out what claim you're trying to strengthen.
- Too many test-takers jump into the answers, unclear of what argument they've been asked to strengthen.

Answer choices
As you read each answer, ask yourself:

- Does this answer help that claim more than the other four answers?

Assume that all five answers are true. The correct answer is a new piece of evidence that supports the claim.

Stronger answers are often better. "Most," for example, is better than "many."

Weaken

Weaken questions are nearly identical to Strengthen questions. But instead of trying to help the author, choose the answer that will hurt the author's argument most. The process is the same: understand, predict, and eliminate.

Prediction
- Go back to the passage to figure out what claim you're trying to weaken.
- Too many test-takers jump into the answers, unclear of what argument they've been asked to attack.

Answer choices

As you read each answer, ask yourself:

- Does this answer hurt that claim more than the other four answers?

Assume that all five answers are true. The correct answer is a new piece of evidence that hurts the claim.

Stronger answers are often better. "Most," for example, is better than "many."

Chapter 19:
Reading Comprehension Core Strategies

Chapter Overview

In this chapter, we'll wrap up all of the information we've covered on Reading Comprehension. We'll start by dispelling the fallacy that you can't get better at Reading Comprehension. Next, we'll offer practical RC strategies such as manufacturing interest and active reading.

Improving Your Reading Comprehension

Many students buy into the myth that they can't improve their Reading Comprehension scores. That myth is false.

How do we know? We've seen students do it over and over again.

Reading Comprehension tests your ability to understand and make accurate inferences from long, poorly written passages. So the key to scoring higher on RC is to get more comfortable navigating and understanding these longer passages. There are relatively few core skills needed to master Reading Comprehension, but you'll have to dig deep into each skill to see improvements.

Ben

    Quick side note. Although RC passages are longer than LR passages, they're not long. If you feel like a 16-sentence passage is long, you're in for a world of hurt. In law school, you'll read 16 sentences before your first sip of coffee every day. So start seeing them for what they are—short, easy warm-ups. You got this.

BREATHE

Never let anxiety push you to move faster or put less care into a passage or question. Approach each passage, question, and sentence with the same calm, cool, and collected mindset. Take a deep breath before you start, and take another whenever you feel anxious. Rushing through the passage in a panic won't save you time because you won't understand what you're reading. So when you need to, take a deep breath to get into the right mindset.

Why does this work? When you take a deep breath, blood is redirected from your amygdala, a region in your brain primarily processing emotion, to your frontal cortex, which processes critical reasoning. A couple of deep breaths can make you better at the LSAT.

STAY FOCUSED

Many students feel that they suffer from lapses in focus during Reading Comprehension, and understandably so. RC requires that students carefully but efficiently read four longer passages under timed pressure, most of which cover topics they know or care little about. When you're starting out, you might lose focus occasionally. Focus is, however, a skill that can be improved. To improve your focus, we recommend you do two simple things:

1. **Mental Reset**

    Ben

        When I was studying for the LSAT, my instructor told me to pause, close my eyes, imagine a blue flame, and wiggle my toes before I started each RC passage. It was weird, so I didn't do it. Looking back, I can recognize the merit of what he was saying.

    Nathan

        Definitely. The goal of that admittedly strange exercise isn't to imagine a blue flame and wiggle your toes; it's to give yourself a mental reset. Your mental reset doesn't have to be that strange, but you should have one. It could be as simple as closing your eyes and taking three deep breaths. Do whatever you have to do to put yourself in a calm, focused mindset before you start each passage.

2. **Talk Back**

Conversing with the author as you read is a great way to read actively. After you read the first sentence, pause, figure out what the passage is about, and ask the author any questions you have. If the passage is about African American poetry during the 1800s, you may ask: What does the author think about this poetry? How did this poetry develop throughout the 1800s? Or what is the lasting cultural significance of this poetry? The author may not answer these questions, but by pausing to question the author, you give yourself time to process, synthesize, and anticipate where the author might go next. You can and should do this any time the author finishes discussing a particular thought or idea.

LEARN TO MANUFACTURE INTEREST

Lawyers make a living reading cases they have no personal interest in. Thankfully, nearly any topic can be interesting if you commit to looking closely enough. As you read, challenge yourself to go deeper to understand what the author is telling you and why.

One effective way to manufacture interest in a topic is to be highly critical. Pretend you're a defense attorney reading the opposing attorney's argument. In that context, you would poke and prod at every piece of evidence they introduce and every argument they make. Start thinking and reading like a lawyer now. Read critically. Be mean to the author if you have to! Remember, RC tests skills you'll use every day in law school. Start practicing those skills now.

MUST BE TRUE MINDSET

On Reading Comprehension, default to treating every question like a Must Be True. The correct answer will be proven by the passage. Each wrong answer will include something that the passage didn't say or even contradicts. As soon as an answer choice makes one of these mistakes, eliminate it.

CATCH THE AUTHOR'S OPINION

It's not enough just to know what the author is saying. You should also find the author's opinion. In rare passages, the author is neutral and shares only information. But usually, the author has an opinion, and at least one question will ask you about it. Key into the author's attitude and pay attention to the adjectives and adverbs the author uses.

Here's an example from the first passage of Section 4 in Test 123.

> Those with knowledge and expertise in multiple areas risk being perceived as lacking any expertise at all, as if ability in one field is diluted or compromised by accomplishment in another. Fortunately, there are signs that bias against writers who cross generic boundaries is diminishing; several recent writers are known and respected for their work in both poetry and fiction.

The word "fortunately" communicates the author's opinion. It tells us that the author thinks decreasing bias against boundary-crossing writers is a good thing.

By the way, if you found yourself rereading the example's mildly awkward first sentence to get oriented, that's a good thing. That's how the best test-takers excel. Don't make the mistake of moving on when you're not exactly sure what you just read. If you made that mistake, stop now, go back, and reread that example until it clicks. Start building this habit now. You can and will understand every sentence on this test—if you try.

Part III:

Tying Up the Loose Ends

Chapter 20
LSAT Writing

Chapter Overview

Students often find out there is a writing section on the LSAT months into their prep and panic. But there's no reason to worry. You can crush the writing sample.

LSAT Argumentative Writing

LSAT Argumentative Writing is a section you complete separately from the other test sections. You can take it up to eight days before your official test. Your score won't be released until it's completed, so you might as well get it out of the way early. The window to take the writing section closes after one year.

Take the writing section seriously. It's not scored, but it's part of your application. Law schools can use it to evaluate whether the rest of your file reflects your true writing abilities.

DON'T STRESS

Your time is best spent preparing for the scored sections. Know what to expect when you complete your writing sample, but don't worry about writing multiple practice essays or extensively reviewing strategies. It's a simple persuasive essay.

PICK A SIDE

In the essay, you'll evaluate an issue and take a position. The prompt consists of background information, a question for debate, and several different perspectives on the issue. Your job is to take a position and defend it.

- You'll have 15 minutes to review the prompt and take notes in the "digital scratch paper" provided. You won't be able to copy and paste from your notes into your essay.
- Use this time to carefully read the material and organize your thoughts.
- You can use your own knowledge, experience, and values to shape your thesis.
- You must address at least one of the perspectives given in the prompt.
- When you're finished reviewing, you'll have 35 minutes to write the essay. You'll have access to the prompt and your notes as you write.

PROOFREAD YOUR ESSAY

The goals are the same as for any good piece of writing. Review the essay when you're finished. Check for errors and ensure it flows well. A strong essay will:

- have a clearly stated thesis
- develop the argument with specific examples
- address potential objections
- be organized logically
- communicate the message effectively
- value quality over quantity

CHECK LSAC'S RULES

For a full list of rules and to make sure your session goes smoothly, be sure to review LSAC's instructions.

STRUCTURING YOUR ESSAY

Begin with a clear, concise thesis statement. A thesis statement should tell the reader your position and set the direction of everything that follows.

Next, explain your reasoning. Support your position with specific examples.

Evaluate at least one of the given perspectives and explain how it connects to your argument. Address potential counterarguments. Show why your recommendation prevails.

Conclude by restating your position.

Nathan

We're serious. It's that simple. You don't need to worry about this writing section for a second until you're already signed up for an official LSAT attempt. As test day is approaching, read through a few official LSAC practice essay prompts, and try writing a test essay under the same conditions as you would when you sit for the actual LSAT Writing exam. Approach this just like you approach the real test: calm, cool, and collected.

Ben

Students often worry way too much about the writing sample, even to the point of studying for it at the expense of studying for the graded portion of the test. Don't make that mistake. Think about preparing for the writing sample after you're ready for the multiple choice.

Chapter 21
Test Day

Chapter Overview

In this chapter, we'll tell you all about test day. We'll start with a basic question: When should I take the LSAT? From there, we'll move on to discuss withdrawing registration, canceling scores, and managing test anxiety. We'll wrap up with a short discussion of remote and in-person testing options.

When Should I Take the Official Test?

Don't register for any official test until your timed practice test scores indicate that you're ready to take it. Essentially: Would my current practice test scores get me into the school I want to attend, at the price I want to pay? Use the LSAT Demon Scholarship Estimator (LSATDemon.com/scholarships) to see how much your potential offers change when your LSAT changes by a few points.

Your practice test scores won't lie. When they're where you want them, go ahead and register for the official test. When they're not where you want them, there's no point registering.

Most students should take ten or more practice tests before they take their first official LSAT.

Withdrawing vs. Canceling

If you registered too soon, that doesn't mean you have to take the test. You can always just withdraw. It's almost always better to do this than taking a test you're unprepared for and canceling your score.

- You can withdraw until midnight (Eastern Time) the day before the test.
- If you withdraw, schools won't know that you even registered for the test.
- If you cancel, they'll know. But one cancellation doesn't matter.
- You have up to six days after the test to decide whether you want to cancel.
- Unless you got really sick or had some emergency mid-test, there's little point to canceling a score once you've already taken the test. If you did better than you thought, you win. If you did as poorly as you thought, you still don't benefit from canceling because schools use only your highest score.
- Plan to take the LSAT at least twice, officially.

Test Anxiety

Almost everyone experiences test anxiety in some form. It's completely normal to experience anxiety around taking the LSAT because the LSAT is a big deal!

But what can you do about it? Throwing up your hands in defeat and lamenting, "I'm just not good at standardized tests" isn't effective. But there are four main things you can do to beat your test anxiety.

1. Be Prepared

One of the best ways to quell test anxiety is to be prepared. This means you should study for as long as you need before signing up for an official test. If you sign up before you are close to scoring what you want, you're doing it backward. You wouldn't buy a home until you were ready. You have to save up first. Once you've saved enough money for a downpayment and secured a stable job, you can start getting serious about buying a house. But not until then. Why would you treat law school and the LSAT any differently? Both your future home and your legal education can cost hundreds of thousands of dollars. Taking shortcuts will cost you dearly. Give yourself the best possible chance to succeed and take comfort in knowing that you've done so.

How do you know you're ready? If you're within a few points of your goal score, you can sign up for the test as long as you keep studying. If you want to be even safer, you can wait until the average score of your last few practice tests is at or above your goal.

2. Practice How You Play

Taking your practice tests seriously is part of being prepared. Take your practice tests in the same environment, or at least close to the same environment you will encounter on test day. Don't allow yourself extra breaks or distractions. Don't treat questions differently than you would on test day. This practice will help you acclimate to the test-taking environment and learn how to solve questions under time pressure.

Nathan

Remember that "no pets" thing from earlier? Still no pets! No phones, no music, nothing you wouldn't have or use if you were taking the real test.

Ben

The exception here is taking individual timed sections. Taking full tests by doing all three or four sections back to back can give you experience for test day. But full tests are harder to review effectively. So you'll most likely benefit from taking and carefully reviewing timed sections, one at a time—typically completing two to four sections over the course of a week and drilling on the remaining days. By all means, take a full test every now and then—maybe once a month—but the bulk of your study should be taking individual timed sections and drilling.

3. Trust Yourself

You've seen scores you're happy with on multiple practice tests, you've reviewed your mistakes, and you've mastered ignoring the clock. Over weeks, months, or maybe even a year or more, you've built the skills you need to succeed, and you've seen your practice test scores rise accordingly. You're ready. Now, it's time to trust yourself. The practice tests you took weren't any easier or harder than the official LSAT you're about to take. The difference between your first LSAT and your highest practice test was you. You made the LSAT easy. You did the work, and now you're good at the LSAT. Get your LSAT swagger on and trust that you are fully prepared to crush it.

4. Take the LSAT at Least Twice

Take some pressure off yourself by planning to take the official test more than once. Pretend you won a chance to win $200,000 by making a single free throw. The rules say that you are allowed up to five attempts. Why would you run up to the free-throw line with just one ball?

Law schools only care about your highest score, so there's no reason not to take the test multiple times unless you get a very high score on your first attempt. The odds here are stacked in your favor. You get five tries, and only your best one matters. Knowing that you have more attempts in the bank and going into the test planning on using them makes each attempt just one of your five tries. If you miss, you've got more shots. Removing that pressure often leads to better performance, which, ironically, makes it less likely that you'll need all five attempts.

Remote vs. In Person

LSAC offers two ways you can take the LSAT. You can take it either remotely (on your own computer) or in person at a testing center. Don't stress too much over this decision—it probably won't matter much.

In general, though, we recommend taking the test at home. Your home allows you to take the test under the same conditions you take your practice tests, which should feel more comfortable. Glitches with proctors and technology do happen from time to time, but we think the benefit of taking it on home turf outweighs the risks. Plus, if anything goes wrong, you may be entitled to retake the test without any penalty. But if you don't have a quiet place or a computer, feel free to use the in-person testing centers.

Before you make the decision, be sure to check out LSAC's policies for technology, testing conditions, and retakes.

Chapter 22
Admissions

Chapter Overview

Once you finish the LSAT, it's time to focus on your application. In this chapter, we'll discuss the frustratingly high costs associated with applying to law school. Then, we'll break down the essential components with "dos" and "don'ts" along the way. We'll explain why you need to apply early and broadly, how to negotiate scholarships, and how to make your final decision. We'll wrap up with Canadian admissions.

Law School Application Costs

It's time for some tough news: Applying to law school is not cheap. After we consider the four main costs, we'll look at how LSAC fee waivers for low-income applicants help.

1. **LSAT Registration Fees**
   $238 per attempt (as of January 2025).

2. **Credential Assembly Service**
   $207. LSAC's Credential Assembly Service (CAS) compiles your GPA, LSAT scores, letters of recommendation, and other application components. You must apply to law schools through the CAS.

$0-20 per transcript. LSAC requires transcripts from every university you've attended. Contact the registrar's office(s) to request them.

3. **Law School Application Fees**
   $0-100 per school. Some schools don't charge application fees, while others charge around $100. Before applying to any school, you should contact the admissions office to ask if they'll waive your fee. They may ask you to fill out a fee-waiver application, which is separate from the LSAC fee waiver discussed below. Their answer may be based on your financial need, grades, or test scores. They'll often say "yes," with no questions asked, because they want you to apply.

4. **LSAC CAS Report Fees**
   $45 per school. You must send each school your CAS report. Some schools may be willing to waive this fee, meaning they pay the fee to LSAC in your place. The added cost for the law school makes CAS report fee waivers less common than application fee waivers. Still, it's worth asking.

LSAC FEE WAIVERS

LSAC offers two tiers of fee waivers. You can find the eligibility requirements for each on its website. There are no penalties if your fee-waiver application is rejected, so if you might be eligible for a fee waiver, apply.

TIER ONE

If you're granted a tier-one fee waiver, you'll get:

- Two LSATs
- One LSAT Writing
- One CAS registration fee
- Six CAS reports
- One-year subscription to LawHub Advantage
  - » Includes access to official LSAT practice tests, an application tracker, and other pre-law resources.
- Score Preview for two LSATs
  - » A test-taker with Score Preview can cancel their score within six days, though they still receive the score at the same time as other test-takers. If you cancel your score, law schools will still be able to see that you took the LSAT, but your score will be hidden. Unless you get Score Preview through a fee waiver, we do not recommend purchasing it.

TIER TWO

If you're granted a tier-two fee waiver, you'll get:

- One LSAT
- One LSAT Writing
- One CAS registration fee
- Three CAS reports
- One-year subscription to LawHub Advantage
- Score preview for one LSAT

Most schools will waive their application fee for fee-waiver recipients. LSAT Demon also offers generous discounts to fee-waiver recipients.

Law School Application Components

Put time and effort into every component of your application. It'd be a shame to spoil a great LSAT score or GPA with a careless application.

PERSONAL STATEMENT

Personal statements are 1–2-page essays about you. Topics vary greatly. We recommend focusing on a meaningful story from your work experience. Your goal is to show the law school that you're a normal, well-rounded person who is capable of doing the work in law school and succeeding in a legal career.

- **Shorter is better.** Write up to two pages but never more, even if the school allows more. A page and a half should be the minimum, but you don't need to pad it with fluff to get to two pages.

- **Cut to the chase.** You don't need a lengthy intro. Grab the reader's attention by diving into your story. And stay on topic; any points that don't directly relate to your story should either be represented somewhere else in your application, such as on your resume, or left out. Don't try to include "everything."

- **Make yourself look good.** Too many applicants use their personal statements to address insecurities directly. For example, if you have a low GPA, ignore the instinct to talk about it here. It will do you more harm than good because it draws more attention to it. You can, however, address a weakness indirectly. For the low GPA example, you could write about an experience you had in your professional career that shows strength in academic skills like research and writing.

- **Instructions can differ from school to school.** Most schools have similar personal statement prompts, but some have different requirements or request different formatting. Be sure to read and fulfill the instructions. Good lawyers read the fine print. Show the school you'll be a good lawyer by jumping through their hoops.

LIVED EXPERIENCE STATEMENT (OPTIONAL)

Lived experience statements, also called diversity statements, are your chance to show an aspect of your background that isn't addressed elsewhere in your application. These essays are optional, but if you have a compelling point to make about how your perspective will contribute to the student body, you should at least attempt to write one. Avoid using this space to trauma dump. You might address a difficult topic if you have a good reason to do so, but address it in a straightforward way.

Below is a sample prompt from the University of Michigan Law School.

> "One of the goals of our admissions process is to enroll students who will enrich the quality and breadth of the intellectual life of our law school community, as well as to expand and diversify the identities of people in the legal profession. How might your experiences and perspectives contribute to our admissions goals?"

Notice that they ask for "experiences." The same basic strategy we suggested for the personal statement—picking a specific anecdote—will go a long way to illustrate your "perspective" here.

RESUME

Tailor your resume for law school. Legal resumes typically stick to one page and are black and white without any pictures or graphics. Your resume should contain your name, full mailing address, phone, and email at the top. List your educational accomplishments in a section titled "Education" with the most recent first. List your work experience in a section titled "Experience" with the most relevant to law first. If everything under Education was a while ago, you might put it after Experience. Lastly, you may include a small section at the bottom containing 2–4 interests. If the school includes any other specific resume instructions, be sure to follow them.

CAS REPORT

Law schools won't review your application until they receive your CAS report from LSAC. Pay the fee or get the law school to pay it, then send the report from the LSAC website. You don't have to do anything else for this component.

LETTERS OF RECOMMENDATION

Law schools typically require 2–4 letters of recommendation (LOR). Younger applicants tend to ask more academic references, while applicants with significant work experience may ask more professional references. Do what makes the most sense for you, but make sure to read the requirements on the application. Some schools may request a certain number of each type.

If you submit academic LORs, ask professors who you know well and who gave you high grades in their classes. It can also be helpful to a LOR writer if you politely ask them to highlight specific strengths about your academic performance, such as engagement in class discussion, research and writing ability, or leadership.

If you submit professional LORs, you can ask your supervisors to highlight academically relevant skills. If you have a client that you know appreciates you, they might be a great candidate to write you a professional LOR.

LSAC offers the option to waive access to view LORs submitted by recommenders. Law schools can see what you choose, so always waive your ability to read them. Failing to do so is seen as a red flag.

OTHER REQUIRED COMPONENTS

Character and Fitness
So you graduate from law school and pass the bar exam. The final step before you can practice law is that you must be admitted to the bar in your state, which requires disclosing your character and fitness history. Serious or repeated run-ins with law enforcement and issues concerning academic integrity can prevent you from ever practicing law, especially if you don't disclose it.

In anticipation of those bar requirements, many law schools require you to disclose character and fitness issues in your application. Read each application closely; some may require you to report a parking violation while others may not. And if the school doesn't ask for your character and fitness history at all, then you don't need to include it.

If you need to explain any character and fitness issues, keep the explanations short and factual. Don't draw unsupported conclusions. Don't make excuses or blame others; take ownership of your actions. Small offenses like a lone underage drinking citation or academic discipline for having a candle in your dorm when you were 20 are typically not a big deal as long as you disclose them. For repeat offenses, a high volume of offenses, or serious offenses, be sure to convey remorse and provide evidenced assurance that the offense will not reoccur.

Most importantly, don't hide anything from the law school. Down the road, if they find out another way, you may be subject to discipline or dismissal from the school. Even worse, you may be unable to practice law if your offenses are serious.

Explaining a Gap
Some schools ask for an addendum to address gaps in work experience and education.

If they don't ask, don't write an addendum; however, you might address a significant gap in another way. Whatever you were doing might be covered in your resume. Or it might fit in with an anecdote that works well for your personal statement or lived experience statement.

Other Required Components
A few schools have additional required essays, like Yale's 250-word essay. Take the opportunity to write about something that adds value and that wasn't specifically covered elsewhere in your application.

PROCEED WITH CAUTION: OTHER OPTIONAL COMPONENTS

Optional Supplemental Essays
Schools often have other optional essay prompts. Only submit optional essays if they add value to your application. Some are meant to be fun, like Georgetown's open-ended option to submit a top-ten list.

Why X School
Some schools invite you to communicate your interest in that particular school.

GPA ADDENDUM (OPTIONAL)

Students often feel the need to write an addendum addressing their grades during college. Think long and hard before submitting a GPA addendum because they often harm the overall message of an application. Students frequently submit unnecessary and even damaging details. If you're not sure whether to submit one, err on the side of caution. If you do write one, keep it short and factual.

Tanya's admittedly exaggerated addendum does more harm than good:

> "During my sophomore year of undergrad, I had a professor who unfairly lowered my grade because I had too many absences. The professor did not warn me and often treated me poorly in class. If I had been treated fairly, I would have gotten an A in that class instead of a B."

Tanya did everything wrong. She failed to take responsibility for her actions and drew unsupported conclusions. Any admissions officer worth their salt would decide she was immature. Not good.

Here's another version of Tanya's situation:

> "The B during my sophomore year of undergrad was due to poor attendance. I take full responsibility for my attendance issues in that class. During my final two years, I had zero unexcused absences."

It's better, but Tanya still isn't doing herself any favors. She's unnecessarily divulging the fact that she had poor attendance—a negative point that the admissions committee would probably not have known otherwise. And she's doing it to explain a B. Not worth the tradeoff; whereas had she gotten an F, she would need to explain it.

There are certainly times a GPA addendum is warranted. Consider Lucia:

> "During my sophomore year, my mother died unexpectedly. My grades went down for a few months while I got her affairs in order and adjusted. By the following year, my grades were back up."

Lucia has a single low point in their grades, and there's an understandable reason for it.

Consider Felix:

> "I have matured since undergrad, when I was focused on my sports responsibilities. My MBA program last year was one of the top in the country, and I finished first in my class. I believe this achievement better represents my law school potential."

In only three sentences, Felix explains why he wasn't focused on academics in undergrad and points to a more recent example of his academic success. It provides additional context about his MBA program that looks good and that an admissions officer may not have known otherwise.

Be strategic. Be concise. Think about your audience. When in doubt, don't submit a GPA addendum.

Other Optional Addenda

Addenda should be used sparingly and should always be short and fact-driven. Be careful what you divulge.

Don't write an LSAT addendum to explain an increase in your score unless a school absolutely requires it. When someone's score dramatically increases, it's not unreasonable to assume they studied and got better at the test; an explanation is unnecessary. Even worse, you may fall into the trap of disclosing LSAT accommodations, which may cause admissions officers to doubt whether or not your LSAT is a good predictor of your law school success. Most law schools don't need or ask for that information, so don't give it to them.

Apply Early, Apply Broadly

APPLY EARLY

You should have your application materials ready when applications open in late August and early September.

Why is it important to apply early? It's simple math. Law schools practice rolling admissions, meaning offers of admission come out as early as September and as late as the week of their orientation. Every person admitted before you occupies a seat that is no longer available to you. Applying early maximizes your chances of admission and scholarships because if you apply early, all of the seats and scholarship resources are available.

Imagine the law school admissions season as a marketplace where schools and applicants trade one thing of value for another. Schools offer legal education, specific career prospects, and, rather dubiously, prestige. Applicants offer money in the form of tuition or prestige for the schools through their LSAT and GPA.

Suppose you're about to purchase a house. You wouldn't show up to the doorstep of just one house and tell the owner, "Please let me purchase this house. If you let me purchase this house, I will pay whatever it takes." That's a losing strategy. If the owner refuses to sell you their house, you've already lost.

Even worse, they may sell you the house for significantly more than what it's worth. Instead, you research many houses, compare their pros and cons, and see which owner will give you the best deal.

That's exactly how you should apply to law school. Apply broadly, get competing offers, and get the best deal possible—ideally a full ride. If you only apply to a few schools, you're begging to get ripped off.

Nathan

It's kind of a messed-up game. Schools charge each student a different price. If any normal business did that, it would offend its customers. But applicants are just so excited to get in that they don't realize the school might try to rip them off.

Ben

We don't want that for you. We don't want you to play their game. We want you to play your own game. In your game, tuition is optional. You get to go to law school for free. If your parents are millionaires who can afford to pay $70,000 per year, good for you. Most people can't do that. We just want what's best for you.

Nathan

We built our whole business on showing you how to do it. We both graduated from law school, and we don't want you to pay $200,000 when you could go for free. So please, crush your LSAT, then apply early and broadly.

APPLY BROADLY

Applying broadly means applying to 10–15 schools. The purpose is to find out exactly how much you're worth in terms of tuition discounts (scholarships). If Wake Forest, ranked 25th, accepts you with a 25% discount, but Texas A&M, ranked 26th, accepts you and offers you a full ride, you will know that Wake Forest badly undervalues you. Apply this principle to 10–15 schools, and you'll have a clear picture of your market value.

You'll also gain bargaining power. You could go back to Wake Forest (or your top choice school) and ask them to up their offer. You have a full-ride offer from one of their top competitors, rankings-wise, to give you confidence in your ask.

To find out which schools will likely give you the best scholarships, check out the free LSAT Demon Scholarship Estimator at lsatdemon.com/scholarships.

Type in your GPA and LSAT, press enter, and scroll until you find consistent full-ride offers. Then enter an LSAT score a few points above yours and see how the game can change if you up your LSAT by just a few points.

The Scholarship Estimator is based on the American Bar Association's (ABA) 509 reports, which each law school is required to submit annually. These reports are available through the Estimator or by searching "[law school] 509." On the first page of the report, under the "First Year Class" section, look at the 75th, 50th, and 25th percentile GPA and LSAT stats. Aim for the 75th percentile LSAT score or higher at your top choice.

Many a high achiever will apply to all 14 schools in the top 14 and sleep well that night thinking they have applied broadly. But don't forget to apply broadly to safety schools, too. The strategy works best when you collect several full-ride offers, even if you really only have one specific school in mind. You might even find that you like how some of those safety schools treat you.

On the third page, under Grants and Scholarships, check out how many of the school's students, percentage-wise, received scholarships. In other words, the generosity of the school also affects your likelihood to get one of those discounts.

ABA-accredited law schools are also required to complete a yearly Employment Summary Report. These reports show what types of jobs last year's graduates got and in which states. If you want to work in New York's big law, you should probably go to a school that sends graduates to New York's big law. If you want to work for the government in Washington DC, it might make sense to pick George Washington University, which is located there and sends the vast majority of its graduates into that market, over a school with a higher ranking but with few grads that have the career you want.

Ben

It's a good time to add a caveat about rankings. Law school rankings are both incredibly important and, well, dumb. Care to elaborate for me, Nathan?

Nathan

Yep. Much like a Paradox question, two things that seem at odds are both true. Rankings and prestige matter a lot in legal hiring, but only to a degree. If you want to work at the public defender's office or for a small- or mid-sized law firm, you don't need to go to a top law school.

Ben

The point here is: Don't put too much emphasis on rankings. Cost is the biggest factor. Job outcomes and location matter, too. All American law schools teach roughly the same curriculum. Don't feel like you have to go to a T14 just because that's what everybody on Reddit says.

Decision Time

SCHOLARSHIP NEGOTIATION

Since you've applied early and broadly, you now have competing offers from several schools. If a school admits you, they want you to choose them. However, that law school is also trying to convince hundreds of other applicants to choose them. So your first offer is likely to be the smallest scholarship package a school thinks you'll accept. Many applicants stop once they've gotten their scholarship offer without seeing that it represents the minimum the school is willing to give.

Scholarships are often, although not always, negotiable. We've seen hundreds of students get schools to up their offers. Here are some tips to improve your odds of a successful negotiation:

SCHOLARSHIP NEGOTIATION TACTICS

- **Improve your LSAT score.** By now, you know not to apply until you have a killer LSAT! However, if you already applied with an LSAT score below the median of your target law schools, improve it. Raising your LSAT score is the best way to make yourself a more appealing scholarship candidate and put you in a stronger negotiating position.
- **Maintain open communication.** Keep lines of communication open with admissions offices by providing straightforward, polite responses to offers and any other communications. This approach allows for ongoing discussions and opportunities to negotiate.
- **Be prepared to walk away.** Understand your worth and be ready to request a higher scholarship amount. Be prepared to decline an offer if it doesn't meet your expectations. You have more bargaining power when you're willing to walk away.

Ben

We've had students turn down an offer after an unsuccessful negotiation just to receive another phone call from that same school with a new, better offer. If you're willing to walk away, you have bargaining power.

Nathan

It's true, but it's not the rule. Most of the time, walking away means not attending that school. But when you know your worth, you'll feel confident walking away.

- **Keep an eye out for "scammerships."** The law school tuition discounting game can get ugly, and there are clear winners and losers. Schools are incentivized to offer attractive applicants massive discounts and less attractive applicants little to no discounts to make up for the lost revenue from the top applicants. We call low scholarship offers "scammerships." Look at some ABA 509 reports to see just how pervasive this behavior is among even the nation's elite law schools. It's a messed up system, but it feels even worse if you're on the losing side.

EXAMPLE SCENARIO

Consider Judy, who's applying to Florida International University and the University of Miami. Suppose FIU offers her a half-tuition scholarship with a decision deadline while Miami places her on a waitlist. Her LSAT score, 160, matches FIU's median but is slightly below Miami's. In this case, Judy's best strategy is to improve her LSAT score, as it's currently not compelling enough for substantial scholarship offers from either school.

Ben

That's right. A half ride isn't substantial. We don't just want you to get in. We want you to go for free.

Nathan

People hesitate to believe us when we say they can go for free, but it's true. In 2023, FIU gave 15% of its 1L class full rides. On the other hand, Miami didn't give any—but that doesn't mean you can't go cheap. Forty-eight percent of their 1L class got somewhere between half and full in the same year. Law schools give a lot of money to candidates with the right LSAT and GPA.

NEGOTIATION TACTICS IN ACTION

If Judy secures a better offer from Miami after accepting FIU's terms, she can politely inform FIU and ask if they're willing to match the new offer. If FIU declines, she has the option to walk away.

Until fully committed, Judy can continue negotiating with FIU, citing financial challenges and requesting a specific increase in scholarship funding. For example, she might say:

> "I'd love to attend FIU, but as I evaluate my finances, I'm struggling to see how to make ends meet. I could meet all my obligations if you'd be open to increasing my scholarship by $7,760 per year. Can this amount be arranged so I can commit now?"

Using a specific number suggests that she's calculated an actual budget. Offering to commit now gives them the certainty they're looking for. Granted, asking for $7,760 might be too little. We're not proposing any particular number. The point is to get ready to play the game that admissions offices play daily.

LEVERAGING OTHER OFFERS

As Judy receives more scholarship offers, she can use them as leverage in negotiations with Miami or other schools. A direct yet courteous approach works well. For instance:

> "I've received an offer from St. Thomas with more favorable financial terms. I'd love to attend Miami. It's my top choice. But I can't justify the difference in cost. Can you match or exceed their offer? Thank you again for your consideration."

CONCLUSION

In short, successful negotiation depends on knowing what you're worth and how to say so nicely. By improving your LSAT score and leveraging other offers, you can ask for and get bigger discounts.

Final Decision

You've done all the hard work. You have a great LSAT score. You've painstakingly put together your best possible application and negotiated scholarships with a few schools. Now, it's time to make your decision.

We recommend you weigh three factors highly:

1. **Cost.** To evaluate costs, pull up each school's 509 report again. Take the total from the Tuition and Fees section, add in the total from the Living Expenses section, and then subtract your scholarship offer. Compare your results for each school. We recommend going where you will have the least cost if it also fits your job outcome and location goals.

2. **Relative Offer Quality.** Look again at the 509 report's Grants and Scholarships section. It breaks down how many students are getting less than half, between half and full, full rides—and some are even getting more than full tuition, which means you can potentially get your living expenses covered, too. Each school also lists their 25th, median, and 75th percentile scholarship amounts. Let's say you're above a school's LSAT and GPA medians, and you see that the school gives out generous scholarships frequently, yet they offered you less than half tuition. You would know that's not a good offer.

3. **Employment Outcomes.** Review the job outcomes again, including locations. Alumni networks are a powerful force in legal hiring, as is general prestige.

4. Sometimes, the right decision is to say no to all the offers. If none of the schools gave you the right offer, be willing to walk away and try again next year. Furthermore, some students find along the way that their career goals don't require law school after all. Do your research, know your value, and you'll be confident in your decision.

5. If you got a full-ride offer at a school of your choice: Congratulations! We're confident that because you prioritized yourself first, it's the beginning of a prosperous legal journey for you.

Canadian Admissions

HOW DO CANADIAN AND AMERICAN LAW SCHOOLS DIFFER?

Price: One significant difference is that sticker price for law school tuition in Canada is about half that of most American law schools (friendly reminder: don't pay that). The flip side is that Canadian schools don't offer as many scholarships—more on this later.

Application process: Canadian law schools don't use LSAC's Credential Assembly Service. Most schools have their own admissions portals. If you're applying in Ontario, including the University of Toronto, Osgoode, or Queen's, you'll use the centralized OLSAS application system.

Just like American law schools, most Canadian ones require your undergraduate transcript, LSAT score(s), letters of recommendation, and personal statement.

- Most law schools in Canada don't accept the GRE as a substitute for the LSAT.
- Quebec law schools don't require the LSAT. But if you've taken it, they will consider your score(s) for better or worse.
- Some schools have language requirements. In Quebec, you must be able to speak French (except for McGill's English-language program).
- More Canadian law schools have specific essay guidelines specifying word limits, formatting requirements, or structure and content guidelines.
- Applicants fall into more categories with different document requirements: general, international, transfer, Indigenous, access, joint-degree, and part-time applicants.
- Some schools request a resume, evidence of eligibility, and letters of good standing.

TL;DR: Read the guidelines on each school's website.

Classes: Like in the U.S., many law schools in Canada use long final exams worth 100% of your grade, particularly in your 1L year. Grades for most classes are determined on a bell curve. Your 1L courses will be mostly predetermined, while your 2L and 3L years will allow more flexibility and electives.

The content of these courses differs from content in the U.S.: Canadian law schools teach Canadian law. If you want to practice law in the U.S., you should study law in the U.S. There are ways to transfer from one country to another, but this often involves another course and another bar exam. The process and regulations vary depending on the province/state you're leaving and the one you're entering. Moving between provinces is much easier than moving between countries—more on this below.

Student life: Canadian and American law schools alike usually offer law clinic experiences. They also have Black Law Students' Associations and other diversity groups, student journals and law reviews, degree specializations like Indigenous law, and other extracurricular opportunities. Class sizes can be smaller than those of big U.S. schools, but student life is usually comparable.

Rankings: Canadian law schools all have similar educational quality and reputation in the job market, lacking an equivalent to the top 14 American law schools. Macleans, the Canadian equivalent of *U.S. News & World Report*, offers a much-discussed ranking of Canadian law schools, but don't give it too much weight. Consider the difference between the highest- and lowest-ranked schools in each country. In the U.S., the difference between Yale and Willamette University College of Law is life-changing. (Have you heard of Willamette? If so, be honest—are you from Salem?) In Canada, the difference between the University of Toronto and the University of Victoria is unremarkable. They both have excellent programs. They have comparable employment outcomes.

HOW DOES BEN AND NATHAN'S ADVICE APPLY TO CANADIAN STUDENTS?

Don't pay for law school—**not applicable.**
Getting a merit-based full-ride scholarship to law school in Canada is rare. Don't go into the application process with this expectation. You can still get a great scholarship, and some schools offer significant financial assistance in 2L or 3L, even if you didn't get any in 1L. Even though tuition is lower in Canada than in the U.S., 10–30k a year still isn't cheap. Just like in the U.S., a better LSAT and GPA in Canada means better scholarship offers. Most law schools offer need-based bursaries, which require a separate application. Canada's tuition assistance model is, in this way, similar to that of Harvard, Yale, and Stanford.

Apply in September or don't apply—**not applicable.**
The deadlines for applying to Canadian schools are much earlier, and many admissions offices don't begin their review process until after the deadline.

Take the LSAT as many times as it takes to get your best possible score—**applicable in some cases.**
Different schools have different policies for interpreting multiple LSAT scores. Some look only at the highest score; U of T and Queen's are examples. Others, like McGill, take an average of your scores. So, think twice before taking the test on a whim. Check each school's website.

Go to school where you want to practice—**generally applicable.**
No matter which country you're in, law school will help you build your professional network. Go to school in the region where you hope to practice. Local connections will help you find job opportunities.

Canadian law schools also gear their curriculum toward helping students be called to the provincial bar. If you attend law school in Nova Scotia, you will be more familiar with the legislation and processes on the Nova Scotia bar than someone who attended school in Saskatchewan. Many provincial bar societies offer province-specific prep courses instead of a bar exam. You can choose which bar exam or course you want to take after graduation. You can find more information on the Canadian Centre for Professional Legal Education website, on the employment pages of law schools, and on the website of the law society of the province you're interested in. These considerations don't preclude you from going to another province to article or to write the bar exam, but you may need to brush up on specific provincial legislation and case law.

If you're a practicing lawyer in one province and want to transfer to another, you can apply for permanent mobility under the National Mobility Act or the Territorial Mobility Act if you're in the Northwest Territories. Transferring to or from Quebec practice is more challenging because Quebec law is based on the Napoleonic Civil Law tradition rather than on the British Common Law tradition. The Interjurisdictional Practice Protocol exists to govern these transfers.

Get the best LSAT score you can—100% applicable.
The LSAT is a significant component of your application in Canada, just as it is in the U.S. Many Canadian schools are transparent about the weight attached to each component of your application, and unsurprisingly, the LSAT always carries a lot of weight. For instance, at UVic, your GPA and LSAT are each weighted at 50%, and your personal statement "may also be taken into account." Don't neglect your personal statement, but understand that if you graduated with a low GPA, knocking your LSAT out of the park is the best way to increase your chances of admission. A strong LSAT score will also greatly increase your chances of getting a merit-based scholarship.

STILL HAVE QUESTIONS?

If you're looking for specific information about a school or program, each law school has a comprehensive admissions page on its website. Most also have FAQ pages. If you can't find an answer, consider asking the admissions office directly. This is the start of your relationship with the people who will read your file, so remember to be professional and thoughtful in your correspondence.

Chapter 23
Testing Accommodations

Chapter Overview

Imagine pushing a shopping cart around your local supermarket. You see many other shoppers. You all need to get milk, eggs, and your favorite cereal, but you notice that your cart has one wheel that doesn't spin quite right. It works, but you have to constantly steer your cart back on track as it wanders off on its own.

For many neurodivergent students, that's how the LSAT can feel. In this chapter, we'll discuss whether and how to get accommodations on the LSAT.

Testing Accommodations

LSAT accommodations are available to anyone with documented disabilities. There is no penalty if your application is denied. So if you think you might be entitled to and benefit from accommodations, apply for them.

To get accommodations, you must register for an official LSAT and then apply through the LSAC website. The application requires supporting documentation.

Available Accommodations
- Extended time (1.5x or 2x time)
- Extra breaks between sections
- Stop and start breaks during each section
- Braille writer, note, or display
- Tactile manipulators
- Excel spreadsheets
- Human reader
- Amanuensis or scribe
- Permission to sit or stand during testing
- Permission to read or speak out loud
- Food permitted at workstation
- Alternative test formats such as paper and pencil
- Extra-large print

Although there are several different types of accommodations, most seek and get extended time. As of the 2022-2023 testing cycle, 65% of all approved accommodations were for extended time.

But be careful what you ask for. Some students ask for double time (2x) thinking that it'll boost their chances of getting time and a half (1.5x). In almost all cases, you get what you ask for, so you'll almost certainly get double time. For some test-takers, 70 minutes per section can be too much time and thus draining. For others, it's exactly what they need and want.

Will Schools Know About My Accommodations?
Not unless you tell them. LSAC isn't allowed to report which students are accommodated or how to law schools. So the schools won't know unless you tell them. We recommend you don't disclose any accommodations until after you are admitted and have put down your deposit for that school. At that point, you can work with the admissions office to implement any accommodations you are entitled to during law school.

Accommodations Can Be Dangerous

Not everyone who can get accommodations should. That decision is up to you. But we've seen students who are granted accommodations early on in their studies, then get so good at the test that the accommodations become an inconvenience. Finishing too early on a section can take you out of your rhythm and hurt your performance. Whether or not you choose to pursue accommodations is entirely up to you, and we'll never criticize you for your decision. Just be aware that accommodations aren't always all that they're made out to be.

Leverage Your Neurodivergence

Neurodivergence can be difficult to navigate, but in some cases, neurodivergence can become a superpower when channeled correctly. For instance, one symptom of ADHD can be difficulty in maintaining focus on any one particular thing. Yet another symptom of ADHD can be hyperfixation. The first won't help you on the LSAT, but the second absolutely can.

Think back to the shopping cart analogy. Once you learn how your shopping cart behaves, you can accomplish the same things as the other shoppers. You'll just have to adjust the way you push your cart. The same can be true with your neurodivergence.

Do some deep digging and self-reflection. Is there anything about the way you think that can be channeled into an LSAT superpower? If so, when is that way of thinking typically activated?

Appendix A:
Closed Question Types

We may have called the theory behind Closed questions "boring" in chapter 12, but to us, it's anything but. Since you made it this far, we're guessing you feel the same. When you're drilling, and you come across a new question type, this is a great place to get some guidance. In the appendices, we're going to repeat ourselves a lot. That's because the LSAT repeats itself a lot.

Must Be True

Since we already discussed this in chapter 12, we'll skip the sample question and get to the nitty-gritty.

Read the following questions. Do you see how they're all asking the same thing? If not, read them again.

- If the statements above are true, which one of the following must be true?
- Which one of the following conclusions follows logically from the statements above?
- Which one of the following can be properly inferred from the passage above?
- Which one of the following can be properly concluded from the mayor's statements?
- The statements above logically commit the executive to which one of the following conclusions?

They all ask you to figure out which answer must be true given what was said in the passage.

MAKING PREDICTIONS

1. Treat everything in the passage as evidence.
Assume that all the statements in the passage are true, even if some of them are not true in the real world. Although the passage could be a full-blown argument with premises and a conclusion, it's usually just a set of facts.

2. Based on that evidence, predict what else must be true.
To figure out what else must be true, examine how each statement in the passage relates to the other statements. Can you combine any of the statements together to infer something new? If the passage tells you that "some cats love ice cream," for example, and that "ice cream is a carcinogen," you should think to yourself that "some cats love a carcinogen." That could be the correct answer. These predictions often feel painfully obvious—and that's a good thing. Don't shy away from predictions that feel obvious.

CHOOSING AN ANSWER

Because there can be several things that must be true, you can't always predict the answer. You might identify one or two inferences but not the one that they have in mind. So as you read each answer, ask yourself: Does this answer have to be true?

The correct answer will either...

1. restate one of the facts in the passage or
2. combine two or more of those facts to infer something new.

When an answer accurately restates a fact in the passage, don't hesitate to select that answer simply because it's a restatement. Even if the question asks you to find an answer that can be "properly inferred," an *inference* is just something that *must be true*. It does not have to be something new. So restatements, which have to be true, are great answers. Pick them and move on. Just make sure that they accurately restate what was said in the passage.

Because we're trying to find something that must be true, the *weaker* the answer, the better. It's easier to prove, for example, that *some* people like ice cream than it is to prove that *most* or *all* people like ice cream. Granted, content is more important than word strength, but be wary of answers that use strong words such as *all, any, each, every, only,* and *most.* These answers could be correct, but they require strong evidence to prove.

Strongly worded phrases, like those used in the examples below, often make answers wrong because they go too far and thus aren't proven by the passage:

- the *most* effective method for treating cancer is
- the *only* way to avoid weight loss is
- the *best* place to be during an earthquake is
- the *primary* purpose of this legislation is
- the *most* important factor in this election is
- the *principal* cause of pollution is

Nathan

I want to offer a strong word of caution here. Many students cause themselves nothing but misery by focusing too much on answer choice strength. I sometimes wonder if we'd be better off not even mentioning it. Answer choice strength can help, as a secondary or tertiary concern. But you'll miss questions if you dismiss every strong answer choice on Closed questions, just like you'll miss questions if you dismiss every weak answer on Open questions. Ben, can you bring this point home for me?

Ben

Absolutely. Strong answers can be correct on Closed questions if the facts justify their strength. And weak answers can be correct on Open questions if there's no better answer. In other words, strong answers need strong support and weak answers need weak support, but word strength doesn't matter in a vacuum. You have to understand what each passage is saying to be able to catch incorrect answers based on word strength. Students who focus primarily on answer choice strength are taking a dangerous shortcut.

TROUBLESHOOTING

If the passage is long and convoluted, compare each answer with only the part of the passage that seems relevant to the answer you're looking at. Comparing an answer to the entire passage can invite you to gloss over key details. Then ask yourself:

- Does this answer have to be true given what the passage says right here?

Granted, you can't ignore the other parts of the passage that might be relevant. But you might need to divide and conquer to see why that answer must be true.

Supported

These questions ask you to figure out which answer is most likely to be true given what was said in the passage:

- Which one of the following is most strongly supported by the information above?
- The statements above, if true, would most strongly support which one of the following?
- If the editorialist's statements are true, they provide the most support for which one of the following?
- Which one of the following best completes the passage?
- Which one of the following most logically completes the argument?

MAKING PREDICTIONS

1. Treat everything in the passage as evidence.
Assume that all the statements in the passage are true, even if some of them are not true in the real world. Although the passage could be a full-blown argument with premises and a conclusion, it's usually just a set of facts.

2. Based on that evidence, predict what else must be true.
To figure out what else must be true, examine how each statement in the passage relates to the other statements. Can you combine any of the statements together to infer something new? If the passage tells you that "most meetings are boring," for example, and that "most meetings are pointless," you might think to yourself, correctly, that "some meetings are both boring and pointless."

CHOOSING AN ANSWER

Because these questions just ask for an answer that is "most strongly supported," the correct answer doesn't strictly have to be true. But in the vast majority of these questions, the correct answer ends up being something that must be true.

That said, even if the correct answer doesn't have to be true, you're still looking for the best answer—the one that is most likely to be true. So as you read each answer, ask yourself:

- Does this answer absolutely have to be true?
- If not, is it at least the one that is most likely to be true?

The correct answer will either...

1. restate one of the facts in the passage or
2. combine two or more of those facts to infer something new.

When an answer accurately restates a fact in the passage, don't hesitate to select that answer simply because it's a restatement. The correct answer does not have to be something new.

In fact, restatements, which have to be true, are great answers.

The correct answer on a Must Be True or Supported question also doesn't have to cover all the information in the passage. As long as it's the answer best supported by some part of the given facts, it's correct.

Because we're trying to find something that is supported by the facts, the weaker the answer, the better. It's easier to prove, for example, that some people like ice cream than it is to prove that most or all people like ice cream. Granted, content is more important than word strength, but be wary of answers that use strong words such as *all*, *any*, *each*, *every*, *only*, and *most*. These answers could be correct, but they rarely have to be true. (But see our caveat above about relying too much on answer choice strength!)

Test 135, Section 4, Q18

Hospitals, universities, labor unions, and other institutions may well have public purposes and be quite successful at achieving them even though each of their individual staff members does what he or she does only for selfish reasons.

Which one of the following generalizations is most clearly illustrated by the passage?

A. What is true of some social organizations is not necessarily true of all such organizations.

B. An organization can have a property that not all of its members possess.

C. People often claim altruistic motives for actions that are in fact selfish.

D. Many social institutions have social consequences unintended by those who founded them.

E. Often an instrument created for one purpose will be found to serve another purpose just as effectively.

Explanation

Yeah, that makes sense. The goal of a hospital is to heal sick and/or hurt people, and it can be good at it even if, hypothetically, each doctor and nurse at the hospital was only in it for the money. Now, there's no flaw in this argument because it says "may," which is very soft, provable language. If I were to take a generalization out of this, it could be something like, "The whole can be one thing even if all of its parts are something different."

A. No, they didn't compare the different organizations. We're looking for a whole-to-part comparison.

B. Yes. A property is a characteristic. An organization is a whole, and each of its members are its parts. This translates to, "a [hospital] can have a [public purpose] that not all of its [staff members] possess." This fits perfectly with the passage and is the whole-to-part comparison we were looking for. This is the right answer.

C. We don't know whether the staff members claimed altruistic motives. Out.

D. We don't know who founded these organizations, what they intended, or what the social consequences are of having selfish staff members. Way off.

E. We never said what the hospitals were created for and we never said they serve another purpose. We're looking for a whole-to-part comparison, and this ain't it.

MUST BE TRUE VS. SUPPORTED QUESTIONS

While a Must Be True question asks for the answer that "must be true," a Supported question just asks for the answer that is "most strongly supported."

Ben

This softer language gives the test-writers a little wiggle room. The correct answer in a Supported question doesn't have to be 100% proven. In most cases, however, it is. Here's the only difference between these two questions:
- If the statements above are true, which one of the following must be true?
- If the statements above are true, which one of the following is most strongly supported?

Nate

In my first five LSAT books, I treated these two question types as one—Must Be True. This is a perfectly acceptable approach because it helps keep your standards high on Supported questions. It's great if you find an answer that's strictly true on a Supported question. Just remember that if you don't find one, the softer language in the question allows you to settle for the next best thing.

Conclusion

These questions ask you to find the main conclusion of the argument:
- Which one of the following most accurately states the conclusion drawn in the argument?
- Which one of the following sentences best expresses the overall conclusion of the surrealist's reasoning?
- The main point of the argument above is that...

MAKING PREDICTIONS

As you read the passage, pause after each sentence to think about what the author is trying to say. Then predict the answer by doing the following:

1. Find the main conclusion in the argument.
The main conclusion is one specific point that the author ultimately tries to prove. It could be stated in the beginning, the middle, or the end. It could be an entire sentence or just part of a sentence.

The rest of the argument will always include at least one piece of evidence that supports the main conclusion.

The conclusion is often the most controversial-sounding statement in the passage. If the argument says that we should do something, ask "why should we?" If the rest of the passage provides evidence for that idea, it's probably the main conclusion of the argument.

2. Restate conclusions that refer back to something else.
When the main conclusion refers back to an idea that was stated earlier in the passage, incorporate that idea into the conclusion as you restate it.

In the argument below, for example, the word "they" in the conclusion refers back to the "scientists" mentioned in the first sentence:

> Joe: Many **scientists** argue that the world is getting warmer. But **they** are wrong. This year's average temperatures are colder than last year's.

What is Joe trying to say? If these scientists are wrong, then Joe is trying to tell us that the world is not getting warmer. That's how you want to restate the conclusion in your own words.

Granted, the clause that "they are wrong" is the main conclusion. But you want to know what that conclusion is actually saying—that is, what the scientists got wrong—before you start looking at the answers.

If the conclusion uses a word like *such*, *this*, or *that*, it's probably referring back to an idea that you need to incorporate into the main conclusion. All these conclusions point back to something that was mentioned earlier:

- We should adopt **this** proposal. (What proposal should we adopt?)
- **That** criticism is unjustified. (What criticism is unjustified?)
- **Such** penalties are too high. (What penalties are too high?)

CHOOSING AN ANSWER

As you read each answer, ask yourself:

- Does this answer restate what I identified as the main conclusion?

Remember, wrong answers often restate premises or give you something that you might infer or conclude from the evidence provided. We're looking for what the author is trying to prove, not just anything that she could prove with the evidence she cites.

TROUBLESHOOTING

If you have trouble finding the main conclusion, do the following:

1. Look for opposing viewpoints.
If the passage begins by telling you what other people believe or claim, the main conclusion will often come right after that claim and reject it.

In the global-warming argument above, the first sentence is an opposing viewpoint, the second is the main conclusion, and the third is a premise. Granted, the main conclusion doesn't have to come right after an opposing viewpoint, but it's pretty common.

2. Watch out for intermediate conclusions.
An intermediate conclusion is a statement that (1) is supported by a premise and (2) supports the main conclusion. Because it supports the main conclusion, it acts as a premise. But it's also a "conclusion" because it's supported by another premise in the argument:

> **Annalisa:** John hates board games, and chess is a board game. **So** he hates chess. **Thus**, John should stop going to chess club.

In the abstract, that's saying:

> **Annalisa:** *Premise*, and *premise*. **So** *intermediate conclusion*. **Thus**, *main conclusion*.

Here, the words *so* and *thus* both introduce conclusions. But "he hates chess" is an intermediate conclusion because it supports the conclusion that "John should stop going to chess club."

Test-takers are more likely to misidentify the main conclusion when the test-writers move the conclusion to the beginning of the passage but use a conclusion indicator such as *therefore*, *thus*, or *so* near the end of the argument:

> **Annalisa:** John should stop going to chess club. John hates board games, and chess is a board game. **Thus**, he hates chess.

In the abstract, the argument looks like this:

> **Speaker:** *Main conclusion. Premise*, and *premise*. **Thus**, *intermediate conclusion*.

Many test-takers mistakenly think that the last sentence is the main conclusion. They get distracted by the "thus" in the last sentence and miss how the last sentence supports the first. To be clear, the last sentence is a conclusion, but it's not the main conclusion. The correct answer would restate the first sentence, not the last.

Keep it simple: treat intermediate conclusions just like premises. If a sentence supports another sentence in the argument, it cannot be the main conclusion.

3. Use argument indicators—but cautiously.

The words *therefore*, *thus*, and *so* come right after a premise and right before a conclusion. But they do not necessarily introduce the main conclusion. As we just saw with the word *thus* in the argument about John's chess club, any of these words could introduce an intermediate conclusion.

Similarly, the words *because*, *since*, and *for* come right before a premise and near a conclusion. That conclusion, however, might not be the main conclusion. It could be an intermediate conclusion.

In short, argument indicators are helpful, but don't automatically assume that they introduce the main conclusion—especially in a Conclusion question.

4. Use the "therefore" test when you see two conclusions.

If you're debating between two conclusions, use the "therefore" test to figure out which is the one and only main conclusion. Here's the test:

State the first conclusion, the word "therefore," and then the second conclusion. If that arrangement makes sense, then the second conclusion is probably the main conclusion.

If that arrangement doesn't make sense, reverse the order by stating the second conclusion, the word "therefore," and then the first conclusion. If this new arrangement makes more sense than the first, then the conclusion that came after "therefore" this time is probably the main conclusion.

In the example below, which arrangement makes more sense?

> Mike likes sharks. **Therefore**, sharks have sharp teeth.
> Sharks have sharp teeth. **Therefore**, Mike likes sharks.

The second one makes more sense, so the main conclusion is "Mike likes sharks."

Test 123, Section 2, Q1

Economist: Every business strives to increase its productivity, for this increases profits for the owners and the likelihood that the business will survive. But not all efforts to increase productivity are beneficial to the business as a whole. Often, attempts to increase productivity decrease the number of employees, which clearly harms the dismissed employees as well as the sense of security of the retained employees.

Which one of the following most accurately expresses the main conclusion of the economist's argument?

A. If an action taken to secure the survival of a business fails to enhance the welfare of the business's employees, that action cannot be good for the business as a whole.

B. Some measures taken by a business to increase productivity fail to be beneficial to the business as a whole.

C. Only if the employees of a business are also its owners will the interests of the employees and owners coincide, enabling measures that will be beneficial to the business as a whole.

D. There is no business that does not make efforts to increase its productivity.

E. Decreasing the number of employees in a business undermines the sense of security of retained employees.

Explanation

It's critical to pause between sentences and make sure you're engaging with the content. In this argument, I stopped after the second sentence and asked, "wait, what? You just said boosting productivity 'increases profits for the owners and the likelihood that the business will survive.' But now you're telling me that 'not all productivity increases are beneficial to the business as a whole?' Why?" As I begin the third sentence, I'm expecting evidence for the claim that was just made. And sure enough, that's exactly what I find. The third sentence is a reason why the second sentence is true. In other words, it's a "premise." This premise supports the second sentence. If we rearranged the second and third sentences, and added "because" and "therefore," it would sound like this:

"Because attempts to increase productivity decrease the number of employees, which clearly harms the dismissed employees as well as the sense of security of the retained employees, therefore not all efforts to increase productivity are beneficial to the business as a whole."

It's a very simple argument, with one premise and one conclusion. Because the third sentence supports the second sentence, the second sentence is the conclusion of the argument.

A and C are misstatements of the argument. D is background information that has no bearing on the logic. E is a premise in support of the argument's main conclusion. The correct answer is B.

Reasoning

These Closed-record questions ask you to describe how the author draws her conclusion:

- Which one of the following most accurately describes the method of reasoning used in the argument?
- The ethicist derives her conclusion by...
- The argument proceeds by...

MAKING PREDICTIONS

Although the passage must be an argument, it doesn't have to be flawed. They're just asking you what kind of reasoning the author is using. Before you read the answers, predict the answer by doing the following:

1. Find the main conclusion.

2. Find the premises.
Separate the premises from everything else. After you find the main point, don't assume that all the other statements are premises. They might include an opposing viewpoint, background information, or a concession.

3. Describe how the premises support the main conclusion.
Your description doesn't need to be perfect. Just look at the reasoning, and

outline what's happening in your own words, in plain English. You might read the argument and say something like this:

> The author refutes a study by showing that its sample is unrepresentative.

CHOOSING AN ANSWER

Don't look at the answers until you've described the argument's reasoning. Then ask yourself:

- Does this answer match my description?
- Does this answer describe exactly what's happening in the passage?

The correct answer must describe exactly what's happening in the argument. If the argument uses one example to support its conclusion, then saying that the argument "relies on multiple examples" would be wrong since it used only one example.

It often helps to break down the answers and read them part by part. As you read each part, ask yourself if that part accurately describes something that's happening in the argument.

It often helps to replace abstract words in the answer with concrete ideas from the passage.

Consider this possible answer:

> The argument proceeds by
>
> **A.** inferring that an attitude would be justified in all situations of a given type on the grounds that this attitude is justified in a hypothetical situation of that type.

In my mind, I'd break this answer into three parts:

> The argument proceeds by
>
> **A.** inferring that an attitude would be justified...
> in all situations of a given type...
> on the grounds that this attitude is justified in a hypothetical situation of that type.

I'd then ask myself these questions as I read each part:

> The argument proceeds by
>
> **A.** inferring that an attitude would be justified... **Is the argument concluding that an attitude would be justified?** *Yes, it is, so I'll keep going.*

in all situations of a given type... **Is that conclusion for all situations of a certain type?** *Yes, it is, so I'll keep going.*

on the grounds that this attitude is justified in a hypothetical situation of that type. **Is it because that attitude is justified in one of those situations?** *Yes, it is, so I'll keep this answer open.*

This answer is correct because it accurately describes what's happening. If you answer "no" to any of these questions, then the answer is wrong.

Test 123, Section 2, Q20
Gamba: Muñoz claims that the Southwest Hopeville Neighbors Association overwhelmingly opposes the new water system, citing this as evidence of citywide opposition. The association did pass a resolution opposing the new water system, but only 25 of 350 members voted, with 10 in favor of the system. Furthermore, the 15 opposing votes represent far less than 1 percent of Hopeville's population. One should not assume that so few votes represent the view of the majority of Hopeville's residents.

Of the following, which one most accurately describes Gamba's strategy of argumentation?

A. questioning a conclusion based on the results of a vote, on the grounds that people with certain views are more likely to vote

B. questioning a claim supported by statistical data by arguing that statistical data can be manipulated to support whatever view the interpreter wants to support

C. attempting to refute an argument by showing that, contrary to what has been claimed, the truth of the premises does not guarantee the truth of the conclusion

D. criticizing a view on the grounds that the view is based on evidence that is in principle impossible to disconfirm

E. attempting to cast doubt on a conclusion by claiming that the statistical sample on which the conclusion is based is too small to be dependable

Explanation

I actually like Gamba's argument. Gamba is like, "Hey, Muñoz, the study you cite is very under-representative. Therefore, it's not enough to draw your conclusion." Gamba should try the LSAT.

Based on the information that Gamba cites, I think Gamba is right. Only a small portion of the members voted on the proposal, and those voters only represent 1% (!) of the population.

The question wants us to identify how Gamba makes his argument. Gamba shows that the evidence for Muñoz argument is probably unrepresentative by bringing more information to bear on the argument. Let's take a look.

A. Nope. This might've been a good argument, but Gamba didn't make it. Gamba never said, "People who oppose a bill are more likely to get out and vote." Gamba said they only represent a small proportion of the population.

B. No, lol. Gamba just doesn't say this. Also, Muñoz's claim isn't supported by statistical evidence. Only Gamba's claim is.

C. Meh. I don't like this. It's kind of true—Gamba doesn't like the conclusion because there's not enough information in Muñoz's premises. But Gamba doesn't say, "Your premises don't guarantee your conclusion." Gamba brings in new information and shows that Muñoz's argument is statistically not great.

D. No. For this to be true, Gamba would've had to say something like, "We can never disprove your evidence." Gamba doesn't say that, and we can disprove Muñoz's evidence. We could look at the data and see if the association really did vote against the proposal.

E. Yep, this is exactly what I predicted. Gamba says that the association only represents 1% of the population and is thus unrepresentative.

Reasoning (Role)

Role questions, a subset of Reasoning questions, ask you to describe what a particular claim is doing in the argument:

- The claim that there is a crisis in journalism plays which one of the following roles in the critic's argument?
- The statement that storms are dangerous serves which one of the following functions in the argument?

- The claim that people sleep better after exercise figures in the argument in which one of the following ways?

MAKING PREDICTIONS

Although the passage must be an argument, it doesn't have to be flawed. They're just asking you what role one of the claims is playing in that argument.

Before you read the answer choices, predict the answer by doing the following:

1. **Find the main conclusion.**
2. **Find the claim that the question is asking about.**
3. **Describe the role of that claim. Is it...**
   - the main conclusion,
   - an intermediate conclusion,
   - a premise,
   - a concession,
   - an opposing viewpoint,
   - or something else?

If you've already found the main conclusion, this step should be straightforward.

If the claim is the main conclusion, for example, you're done. If it's something else, figure out how it relates to the main conclusion.

If the claim helps the main conclusion, it's either a premise or an intermediate conclusion.

If the claim hurts the main conclusion, then it's either a concession or an opposing viewpoint.

If it's doing something else, describe what it's doing.

CHOOSING AN ANSWER

Don't look at the answers until you've described the role. Then ask yourself:

- Does this answer match my description?
- Does this answer describe exactly what's happening in the passage?

The correct answer must describe exactly what's happening in the argument. If the claim you found is the main conclusion, for example, but the argument also has an intermediate conclusion, then saying it is "the author's only conclusion" would be wrong since it's not the only conclusion in the argument.

It often helps to break down the answers and read them part by part. As you read each part, ask yourself if that part accurately describes something that's happening in the argument. To answer that question, you often have to replace abstract words in the answer with concrete ideas from the passage.

Consider this possible answer:

> **B.** It is a premise that, in conjunction with another premise, is intended to support the argument's conclusion.

In my mind, I'd break this answer into three parts:

> **B.** It is a premise that,...
> in conjunction with another premise,...
> is intended to support the argument's conclusion.

I'd then ask myself these questions as I read each part:

> **B.** It is a premise that,... **Is it a premise?** *Yes, it is, so I'll keep going.*
>
> in conjunction with another premise,... **Is it working with another premise?** *No, it isn't, so I'll stop reading the answer and cross it out.*
>
> is intended to support the argument's conclusion. **No need to even read this part.** *I've already crossed out the answer.*

One bad apple spoils the whole barrel. This answer is wrong because the premise wasn't working with another one.

If and only if you say yes to every part, then that answer is correct. Otherwise, it's wrong.

Test 123, Section 2, Q11

It is now a common complaint that the electronic media have corroded the intellectual skills required and fostered by the literary media. But several centuries ago the complaint was that certain intellectual skills, such as the powerful memory and extemporaneous eloquence that were intrinsic to oral culture, were being destroyed by the spread of literacy. So, what awaits us is probably a mere alteration of the human mind rather than its devolution.

The reference to the complaint of several centuries ago that powerful memory and extemporaneous eloquence were being destroyed plays which one of the following roles in the argument?

A. evidence supporting the claim that the intellectual skills fostered by the literary media are being destroyed by the electronic media

B. an illustration of the general hypothesis being advanced that intellectual abilities are inseparable from the means by which people communicate

C. an example of a cultural change that did not necessarily have a detrimental effect on the human mind overall

D. evidence that the claim that the intellectual skills required and fostered by the literary media are being lost is unwarranted

E. possible evidence, mentioned and then dismissed, that might be cited by supporters of the hypothesis being criticized

Explanation

Pedantic Loser argues that electronic media are probably just changing the way we think rather than making us stupider. Why? See, back when books were invented, some cranks complained that they made us stupider too, since before that Pericles and Socrates had to memorize long speeches and debate each other in ancient Greek forums and stuff.

P.L. let all the books go to his head. Socrates and Pericles probably were way smarter than us, and books totally could have made us stoopider. Without this support, the tech argument is toast.

The question asks us what role the reference to the cranks who complained about books plays in the argument. You have to sort this out before going into the answer choices. As we predicted, this is the evidence (a supposedly analogous situation) that P.L. gives to argue that tech probably isn't making us dumber.

A. No, this is the opposite of P.L.'s argument.
B. That "intellectual abilities are inseparable from the means of communication" is not the general hypothesis of the argument, so no.
C. Yes. Think of this as a Must Be True question. This is a perfect, conservatively worded answer. P.L. argues that tech probably isn't having a net negative effect because books didn't have a net negative effect.
D. This turns the volume up too high. The argument never goes so far as to say that the opposing position is "unwarranted," nor does it claim that those opposed think literary skills are being "lost."
E. This evidence isn't dismissed. There would literally be no support for the argument if it was.

Flaw

These questions ask you to find the answer that describes one of the flaws in the argument:

- Which one of the following most accurately describes a flaw in the argument?
- Which one of the following most accurately describes the reporter's error in reasoning?
- The argument above is most vulnerable to criticism on the grounds that it...
- The reasoning in the argument is questionable because the argument...

MAKING PREDICTIONS

The test-writers are telling you that this argument is flawed, so there must be something wrong with it. Ideally, you'll have already pinpointed at least one problem. But if not, take a moment to find one. Here's how:

1. **Find the main conclusion.**
2. **Find the premises.**
   - Separate the premises from everything else. After you find the main point, don't assume that all the other statements are premises. They might include an opposing viewpoint, background information, or a concession.
3. **Figure out why the premises don't prove the main conclusion.**
   - You have to accept the premises as true. But even when you do, they still won't prove the conclusion. Why don't they?
   - Focus on exactly what the argument is saying to avoid subconsciously helping it. You don't want to make the very assumptions that the test-writers are inviting you to make. Your job is to catch those assumptions and call them out.
   - Many arguments have more than one problem. The more you notice, the better. But after you spot one or two serious ones, you're ready to read the answers.

CHOOSING AN ANSWER

The correct answer will describe exactly what the argument does wrong. So if you can't answer yes to both of these questions, that answer is wrong:

> Does this answer describe something that's happening in the argument? If so, is this a problem for this particular argument?

The correct answer must describe exactly what's happening in the passage. So make sure that every word in the answer ties back to something happening in the argument. To tie the words back, you often have to replace abstract words in the answer with concrete ideas from the passage. If an answer says that the argument "confuses a necessary condition with a sufficient condition," for example, you should be able to identify the necessary condition in the argument. If there's no necessary condition, that answer is wrong.

It often helps to break down the answers and read them part by part. As you read each part, ask yourself if that part accurately describes something that's happening in the argument.

Check your answer by asking: "If I fixed this flaw, would that significantly help this argument?" If it would, then that answer is probably correct.

UNDERSTANDING COMMON ANSWERS

When an answer starts with "takes for granted" or "presumes, without providing justification," treat that answer as a necessary assumption. In general, when these answers are strongly worded, they don't need to be assumed and are thus wrong.

When an answer starts with "fails to consider the possibility" or "ignores the possibility," treat that answer as an answer that's trying to weaken the argument. If it would weaken the argument, then it's probably the correct answer. In general, when these answers are weakly worded, they don't do much to weaken the argument and are thus wrong.

Test 123, Section 2, Q4

Consumer: The latest Connorly Report suggests that Ocksenfrey prepackaged meals are virtually devoid of nutritional value. But the Connorly Report is commissioned by Danto Foods, Ocksenfrey's largest corporate rival, and early drafts of the report are submitted for approval to Danto Foods' public relations department. Because of the obvious bias of this report, it is clear that Ocksenfrey's prepackaged meals really are nutritious.

The reasoning in the consumer's argument is most vulnerable to criticism on the grounds that the argument

A. treats evidence that there is an apparent bias as evidence that the Connorly Report's claims are false

B. draws a conclusion based solely on an unrepresentative sample of Ocksenfrey's products

C. fails to take into account the possibility that Ocksenfrey has just as much motivation to create negative publicity for Danto as Danto has to create negative publicity for Ocksenfrey

D. fails to provide evidence that Danto Foods' prepackaged meals are not more nutritious than Ocksenfrey's are

E. presumes, without providing justification, that Danto Foods' public relations department would not approve a draft of a report that was hostile to Danto Foods' products

Explanation

"You're biased, so you're wrong" is a common logical fallacy on the LSAT. Watch out for this one—you're sure to see it again.

Flaw questions are about finding the one answer that correctly describes something the argument did wrong. You can think of it in two parts: First, the argument must definitely have done this thing you're accusing them of doing. Second, it must be wrong, logically, to do it.

We can eliminate answers that the argument didn't do. We can also eliminate answers that the argument did do but that it wasn't wrong of it to do.

- A. Yep. The argument did treat evidence of bias as evidence that the content of the report is false. "You're biased, so you're wrong." It's a problem that they did this, because it's totally possible that the content of the report is perfectly accurate despite the bias. This is the answer.
- B. No. We have no evidence that the argument relied on an unrepresentative sample.
- C. I suppose the argument did "fail to take into account" this possibility—these arguments aren't infinitely long, so every one of them leaves out infinite things—but why does it matter? Who cares if there's more bias on one side or the other? The entire point of this question is that bias doesn't matter. The report can still be correct no matter how much bias there is on either side.
- D. Again, the argument did "fail to take into account" this possibility. But so what? Danto Foods' prepackaged meals could be entirely devoid of nutrition without changing this argument whatsoever. The argument was about the nutritional value of Ocksenfrey's meals, not Danto's.
- E. It's not fair to say that the argument made this presumption. The argument was about a report on Ocksenfrey's meals, not Danto's.

The correct answer is A because it's the only one that the argument (1) did, (2) wrong.

Necessary Assumption

These questions ask you to find an assumption that the author must agree with:

- Which one of the following is an assumption on which the scientist's argument depends?
- The conclusion relies on which one of the following assumptions?
- The argument presupposes which one of the following?
- The university president's argument requires the assumption that...
- The conclusion does not follow unless...

MAKING PREDICTIONS

Because valid arguments don't make assumptions, there must be something wrong with the argument. Ideally, you've already pinpointed at least one problem. But if not, take a moment to find one. Here's how:

1. Find the main conclusion.

2. Find the premises.
Separate the premises from everything else. After you find the main conclusion, don't assume that all the other statements are premises. They might include an opposing viewpoint, background information, or a concession.

3. Figure out why the premises don't prove the main conclusion.
You have to accept the premises as true. But even when you do, they still won't prove the conclusion. Why don't they?

Focus on exactly what the argument is saying to avoid subconsciously helping it. You don't want to make the very assumptions that the test-writers are trying to hide. Your job is to catch those assumptions.

Many arguments have more than one problem. The more you notice, the better. But after you spot one or two serious ones, you're ready to read the answers.

CHOOSING AN ANSWER

Because there can be several necessary assumptions, you can't always predict the answer. You might identify one or two necessary assumptions, but not the one they have in mind. So as you read each answer, ask yourself:

- Does the author absolutely have to agree with this answer?
- If this answer weren't true, would it destroy the conclusion?
- If you answer yes to either question, that answer is probably correct.

Because we're trying to find something that "must" be assumed, the weaker the answer, the better. To avoid going too far, we want the answer to be as weak as possible. Content is more important than word strength, but be wary of answers that use strong words such as all, any, each, every, only, and most. These answers could be correct, but they rarely have to be true.

Test 123, Section 3, Q9

Naturalist: The recent claims that the Tasmanian tiger is not extinct are false. The Tasmanian tiger's natural habitat was taken over by sheep farming decades ago, resulting in the animal's systematic elimination from the area. Since then naturalists working in the region have discovered no hard evidence of its survival, such as carcasses or tracks. In spite of alleged sightings of the animal, the Tasmanian tiger no longer exists.

Which one of the following is an assumption on which the naturalist's argument depends?

A. Sheep farming drove the last Tasmanian tigers to starvation by chasing them from their natural habitat.

B. Some scavengers in Tasmania are capable of destroying tiger carcasses without a trace.

C. Every naturalist working in the Tasmanian tiger's natural habitat has looked systematically for evidence of the tiger's survival.

D. The Tasmanian tiger did not move and adapt to a different region in response to the loss of habitat.

E. Those who have reported sightings of the Tasmanian tiger are not experienced naturalists.

Explanation

There was a subtle switch between the first two sentences I missed on my first read-through. The first sentence, which is also the conclusion, talks about extinction. Extinction means that something is gone from the face of the

Earth. The second sentence, which supports the conclusion, mentions the tiger's "natural habitat." See the switch? Just because an animal is not in its natural habitat does not mean it was wiped off the face of the Earth.

There's another flaw in the passage, though. The author says that because naturalists haven't found evidence that proves the tiger's existence, tigers must not exist. That's far less of a crime than the first flaw above. Still, it's a flaw nonetheless. What if the naturalists are looking in the wrong spot? Lack of evidence for the existence of something doesn't prove it doesn't exist. Like, really? They looked everywhere?

This is a Necessary Assumption question. I spotted two flaws that point to possible necessary assumptions. The author must agree that "loss of natural habitat" equals "extinction," and "lack of evidence something exists" equals "evidence that thing doesn't exist." If the author disagrees with either of those, the argument falls apart.

As we look through answer choices, just remember: We want something the author has to agree with. Let's see.

- A. We don't care why or how sheep farming drove the tiger to extinction. We just care about whether the tiger is extinct or not. Must this be true for the conclusion to be correct? No. Anything could have driven the tigers to extinction, and the conclusion would still be correct.
- B. Again, our standard on Necessary Assumption questions is: does the author have to agree with this? The author doesn't have to agree with B. What if there is something else hiding the carcasses and tracks, such as rising tides?
- C. "Every" is not the type of language we want to see in Necessary Assumption questions. We want weak language, not strong. If all but one naturalist looked for the tiger's survival, answer C is wrong. That is why we look for weak language on these questions.
- D. Perfect! This was the first flaw we spotted. The argument gave ample evidence that the tiger is not in its natural habitat. But, the author argues that the tigers are extinct. If we negated answer D, saying that the tiger moved to another habitat, we would destroy the conclusion. This is the answer.
- E. What if they're experienced naturalists? Would that completely ruin the argument? No, of course not. The evidence talked about hard evidence, such as carcasses and tracks, when it talked about the naturalists. A sighting does not seem to qualify as hard evidence. This doesn't need to be true.

Disagree/Agree

These questions ask you to find something that two people disagree or agree about. Agree questions are rare, so we'll focus on Disagree questions. When you come across an Agree question, use the same process, but remember you're looking for a point in common between the two people rather than a point on which they disagree.

The following questions are all asking the same thing:

- The statements above provide the most support for holding that Mark and Simon disagree about whether...
- The main point at issue between Michael and Stan is whether...
- Komal's and Sonali's remarks provide the most support for holding that they disagree about whether...
- On the basis of their statements, the two students are committed to disagreeing over...
- The dialogue most supports the claim that Michael and Samantha are committed to disagreeing with each other about the truth of which one of the following statements?

MAKING PREDICTIONS

Ideally, you already see how they disagree. But if not, find something. Read each person's statement carefully and take note of what opinions they have, and what they treat as true. These are all things they believe. If person A believes one thing, and person B believes the opposite, you've found the disagreement.

1. Treat everything in each argument as evidence.
Assume that all the statements in each argument are true, even if some of them are not true in the real world. We just want to know what each person believes, even if they're wrong or their logic sucks.

2. Try to figure out how the two people disagree.
Be careful. The second person might not disagree with the first person's main conclusion, so don't assume that's the issue. Test-takers often read too much into the vague phrase "I disagree." Cool, but with what?

> Jim: We should pull our troops out of the Persian Gulf because it's too hot there.
>
> Sarah: I disagree. The weather there is quite nice.

In this exchange, Sarah is not disagreeing with Jim's conclusion—that we should pull out our troops—but with his premise—that it's too hot there. For all we know, she might agree that we should pull out our troops. We have no clue.

CHOOSING AN ANSWER

As you read each answer, ask what the first person thinks of that answer, and then ask what the second person thinks of that answer. These are two separate questions.

Focus on only one person at a time:

- Does Jim agree or disagree with answer A? Or is it unclear?
- Does Sarah agree or disagree with answer A? Or is it unclear?

If one person agrees with an answer and the other person disagrees with that answer, then that answer is correct.

If both agree with an answer, then it's wrong.

If both disagree with an answer, then it's wrong. Even though they both disagree with the answer, they agree with each other. We want one to agree with the answer and the other to disagree.

If one person doesn't say enough for you to know what that person thinks about an answer, then that answer is wrong and you can move on without evaluating what the other person thinks.

Keep asking those two questions for each answer.

Occasionally, the LSAT includes questions that ask us what the speakers agree on instead of what they disagree on. This is lawyer stuff! Those three letters, "dis," matter a lot. Read carefully. If they're asking you what the two speakers agree on, follow the same strategy—separate your analysis by evaluating each person individually—but then look for an answer that they both agree with.

Test 123, Section 3, Q7

Antonio: One can live a life of moderation by never deviating from the middle course. But then one loses the joy of spontaneity and misses the opportunities that come to those who are occasionally willing to take great chances, or to go too far.

Marla: But one who, in the interests of moderation, never risks going too far is actually failing to live a life of moderation: one must be moderate even in one's moderation.

Antonio and Marla disagree over

- A. whether it is desirable for people occasionally to take great chances in life
- B. what a life of moderation requires of a person
- C. whether it is possible for a person to embrace other virtues along with moderation
- D. how often a person ought to deviate from the middle course in life
- E. whether it is desirable for people to be moderately spontaneous

Explanation

Antonio says that it's possible to live a life of moderation by never deviating from the middle course. Then he mentions some downsides of doing that.

Marla says that never deviating from the middle course is actually not living a life of moderation. If you never risk going too far, she says, you are failing to be moderate in your moderation. It's an interesting idea, don't you think? In Marla's world, one can become an extremist via radical moderation.

We're asked to identify a point of disagreement between the two speakers. I've already done it. They're arguing about whether pure moderation can properly be described as "living a life of moderation."

- A. The two speakers seem to agree that people should occasionally take great chances.
- B. Yep. Antonio describes a life of moderation as one with no deviations. Marla says that's not actually a life of moderation. This is their point of contention.

C. Neither speaker mentions whether it's possible to embrace other virtues alongside moderation.
D. The two speakers seem to agree that the proper amount of deviation is not zero.
E. Both speakers seem to agree that some spontaneity—or at least risk-taking—is desirable.

Parallel (Reasoning)

These questions ask you to find another argument that uses the same reasoning as the argument in the passage:

- Which one of the following is most closely parallel in its reasoning to the reasoning in the argument above?
- Which one of the following arguments is most similar in its pattern of reasoning to the argument above?

MAKING PREDICTIONS

The passage must be an argument. It may or may not be flawed.

Before you read the answers, predict the answer by doing the following:

1. Find the main conclusion.

2. Find the premises.
Separate the premises from everything else. After you find the main point, don't assume that all the other statements are premises. They might include an opposing viewpoint, background information, or a concession.

3. Restate the argument in general terms.
Example:

> Martha: Our profits might drop. If they drop, we must buy more advertising or cut costs. We have already cut costs as much as possible. So if profits drop, we must buy more advertising.

General prediction:

> Something might happen. If that thing happens, then we must do one of two options. We can't do one of those options. So if that thing happens, we have to do the other option.

If restating the argument in general terms is too challenging, try coming up with your own parallel argument instead. Keeping things concrete can help:

> My phone might die. If it does, I must hitchhike or walk. I'm not going to hitchhike. So if my phone dies, I must walk.

ANSWER CHOICES

Don't look at the answers until you've mapped out the reasoning. Then ask:

- Does this answer use the same kind of reasoning?

Look for the same number of premises and conclusions, but not necessarily in the same order. Because their order can change, make sure you're comparing premises to premises and conclusions to conclusions. You don't want to compare the main conclusion in one of the answers to a premise in the original argument.

Although the correct answer often talks about something entirely different, look for the same number of ideas in the same parts of the argument. In the example above, there were three core ideas:

- Dropping profits—appeared twice in the premises and once in the conclusion
- Buying more advertising—appeared once in the premises and once in the conclusion
- Cutting costs—appeared twice in the premises

So the correct answer is likely to have three, albeit different, core ideas distributed throughout the premises and the conclusion in the same way.

The correct answer will almost always use logical terms that mean the same thing as the logical terms used in the original argument. The correct answer might use "usually" instead of "most," for example. Or it might use assert instead of argue. Here are some of the logical terms in Martha's argument:

> Martha: Our profits might drop. If they drop, we must buy more advertising or cut costs. We have already cut costs as much as possible. So if profits drop, we must buy more advertising.

The correct answer has to be the most parallel but might not be perfectly parallel. When you're trying to decide which parts of the argument are more important to match, consider this rough logical hierarchy—from most important to least important:

1. Conditional Statements
2. Some, Most, and All

3. Relative vs. Absolute
4. Correlation vs. Causation
5. Beliefs vs. Facts
6. Should vs. Can vs. Will

When the test-writers ask you for "parallel reasoning," they're asking you to find an argument that uses the same kind of logic to justify its conclusion, even if the topics are different. In the two (mostly) parallel arguments below, I've highlighted some of the underlying concepts that parallel each other.

Original:

> Every competitor on Saturday will either give up or request help, but not both. Those competitors who give up will get a participation award. But those who request help will get an achievement award. Therefore, every competitor on Saturday will get an award.

Parallel:

> All the cows on Jon's farm tomorrow will graze the pasture outside or stay inside all day. The cows that graze the pasture will get unusually sleepy. The other cows will not eat their normal dinner. So all the cows on Jon's farm tomorrow will do something unusual.

The correct answer here is not perfectly parallel, but it's close enough. The goal is to look for the argument that is "most parallel," and this argument has several important similarities, even if they seem different on the surface.

Here's my take on this correct answer:

The first premise and the conclusion both use the word "all," but that means the same thing as the word "every" in the original.

The first premise does not say "but not both," but that's okay because it's impossible to "stay inside all day" and to "graze the pasture outside." So the cows have to do one or the other, but not both.

"Getting unusually sleepy" is different from "getting a participation award," but that doesn't matter. The point is that something happened to the first group and something similar happened to the second group, just as in the original argument. Here, both groups of cows did something unusual.

Referring to the second group as "the other cows" rather than "the cows that stay inside all day" is slightly different, but still logically parallel because all the cows will do one thing or the other.

The conclusion refers back to all the cows, just as the original conclusion refers back to every competitor.

Test 135, Section 1, Q6

Evan: I am vegetarian because I believe it is immoral to inflict pain on animals to obtain food. Some vegetarians who share this moral reason nonetheless consume some seafood, on the grounds that it is not known whether certain sea creatures can experience pleasure or pain. But if it is truly wrong to inflict needless suffering, we should extend the benefit of the doubt to sea animals and refrain from eating seafood.

Which one of the following most closely conforms to the principle illustrated by Evan's criticism of vegetarians who eat seafood?

A. I do not know if I have repaid Farah the money she lent me for a movie ticket. She says that she does not remember whether or not I repaid her. In order to be sure that I have repaid her, I will give her the money now.

B. It is uncertain whether all owners of the defective vehicles know that their vehicles are being recalled by the manufacturer. Thus, we should expect that some vehicles that have been recalled have not been returned.

C. I am opposed to using incentives such as reduced taxes to attract businesses to our region. These incentives would attract businesses interested only in short-term profits. Such businesses would make our region's economy less stable, because they have no long-term commitment to the community.

D. Updating our computer security system could lead to new contracts. The present system has no problems, but we could benefit from emphasizing a state-of-the-art system in new proposals. If we do not get new customers, the new system could be financed through higher fees for current customers.

E. Isabel Allende lived through the tragic events of her country's recent history; no doubt her novels have been inspired by her memories of those events. Yet Allende's characters are hopeful and full of joy, indicating that Allende's own view of life has not been negatively marked by her experiences.

Explanation

Our prediction coming in could be something like, "Even if we don't know whether X is bad, we should give the benefit of the doubt and assume it is to avoid being morally wrong."

- A. This sounds pretty good off the bat. "I'm not sure if I've repaid Farah yet. So, I should assume I didn't and repay her just in case." We're extending the benefit of the doubt to Farah that we haven't paid her in order to avoid doing something morally wrong—not paying your debts obviously isn't good. This will be the right answer.
- B. This conclusion is about something we should expect. Where's the extending the benefit of the doubt to someone? Not feeling this.
- C. Whiff. Being opposed to something isn't extending the benefit of the doubt to avoid being morally wrong.
- D. Nothing potentially morally wrong going on here, just a new computer system.
- E. Allende hasn't been negatively affected by past experiences, so what? Again, no giving the benefit of the doubt and nothing morally wrong going on here.

Parallel (Flaw)

These questions ask you to find another argument that makes the same mistake in its reasoning as the argument in the passage:

- Which one of the following exhibits the flawed reasoning most similar to the flawed reasoning above?
- The questionable reasoning above is most similar in its reasoning to which one of the following?

MAKING PREDICTIONS

The test-writers are telling you that this argument is flawed, so there must be something wrong with it. Ideally, you've already pinpointed at least one problem. But if not, take a moment to find one and articulate it in general terms. Here's how:

1. **Find the main conclusion.**
2. **Find the premises.**
Separate the premises from everything else. After you find the main point,

don't assume that all the other statements are premises. They might include an opposing viewpoint, background information, or a concession.

3. Figure out why the premises don't prove the main conclusion.

You have to accept the premises as true. But even when you do, they still won't prove the conclusion. Why don't they?

Focus on exactly what the argument is saying to avoid subconsciously helping it. You don't want to make the very assumptions that the test-writers are trying to hide. Your job is to catch those assumptions.

Many arguments, by the way, have more than one problem. The more you notice, the better. But after you spot one or two serious ones, you're ready to restate the flaw in general terms.

Consider Ryan's argument:

> Ryan: Most cats are pets. Most pets go to a veterinarian doctor at least once every year. So at least some cats go to a doctor at least once every year.

Even though most cats are pets and most pets go to the vet at least once a year, it's possible that 49% of all pets never go to the vet. And maybe all the cats that are pets fall into that 49%. Heck, maybe only dog owners take their pets to the vet.

To be sure, we don't know that all those cats that are pets fall into that 49% of pets who never make it to the vet. We don't even know that 49% of pets never make it. But because those two situations are both possible, given what the premises say, the conclusion isn't proven. So this argument is flawed.

By the way, the second premise talks about a "veterinarian doctor" and the conclusion talks about a "doctor." That's not a problem, though, because if a cat goes to a "veterinarian doctor," then it has gone to a "doctor."

Granted, if these two phrases had been reversed, it would've been a problem. If a cat goes to a "doctor," it hasn't necessarily gone to a vet. Maybe it went to your family doctor. Strange, but possible.

4. Restate the flaw in general terms.

Example:

> Ryan: Most cats are pets. Most pets go to a veterinarian doctor at least once every year. So at least some cats go to a doctor at least once every year.

General prediction:

Just because most of one thing are a second thing and most of the second thing do X, that doesn't mean that some of the first thing do X. Maybe all of the first thing fall into the 49% of the second thing who don't do X.

To keep things simple, I dropped the timeframe "at least once a year." But the correct answer could talk about a timeframe and that timeframe could be different. It might say something like "at least twice a month."

Either way, the main flaw here is going from most pets go to the vet to some cats that are pets go to the vet. So as long as we see that jump in the answer, that's probably correct.

Parallel Flaw questions want us to match the flaw more than anything else. And when there's more than one flaw, it's more important to match the most serious flaw than the other flaws. Granted, the more you can match, the better. But if an answer is missing the most serious flaw, that's a problem.

If restating the flaw in general terms is too challenging, try coming up with your own parallel flaw instead. Keeping things concrete can help:

Just because most New Yorkers are Democrats and most Democrats support unions, that doesn't mean that some New Yorkers support unions. Maybe all New Yorkers fall into the 49% of the Democrats who don't support unions.

CHOOSING AN ANSWER

Don't look at the answers until you understand why the passage is flawed. Then ask:

- Does this answer have the same flaw?
- Does this answer use the same kind of reasoning?

Look for the same number of premises and conclusions, but not necessarily in the same order. Because their order can change, make sure you're comparing premises to premises and conclusions to conclusions. You don't want to compare the main conclusion in one of the answers to a premise in the original argument.

Although the correct answer often talks about something entirely different, look for the same number of ideas in the same parts of the argument. In the example above, there were three core ideas:

- Cats—appeared once in the premises and once in the conclusion
- Pets—appeared twice in the premises
- Doctor—appeared once in the premises and once in the conclusion

So the correct answer is likely to have three, albeit different, core ideas distributed throughout the premises and the conclusion in the same way. By the way, you could split "doctor" into two sub-ideas: "veterinarian doctor" and "doctor." The first one is a subset of the second, and I bet the correct answer might do something similar: "space museum" and "museum," for example.

The correct answer will almost always use logical terms that mean the same thing as the logical terms used in the original argument. The correct answer might use usually instead of most, for example. Or it might use assert instead of argue. Here are some of the logical terms in Ryan's argument:

> Ryan: Most cats are pets. Most pets go to a veterinarian doctor at least once every year. So at least some cats go to a doctor at least once every year.

The correct answer has to be the most parallel but might not be perfectly parallel. When you're trying to decide which parts of the argument are more important to match, consider this rough logical hierarchy—from most important to least important:

1. Conditional Statements
2. Some, Most, and All
3. Relative vs. Absolute
4. Correlation vs. Causation
5. Beliefs vs. Facts
6. Should vs. Can vs. Will

Test 135, Section 1, Q11
Inspector: The only fingerprints on the premises are those of the owner, Mr. Tannisch. Therefore, whoever now has his guest's missing diamonds must have worn gloves.

Which one of the following exhibits a flaw in its reasoning most similar to that in the inspector's reasoning?

A. The campers at Big Lake Camp, all of whom became ill this afternoon, have eaten food only from the camp cafeteria. Therefore, the cause of the illness must not have been something they ate.

B. The second prototype did not perform as well in inclement weather as did the first prototype. Hence, the production of the second prototype might have deviated from the design followed for the first.

C. Each of the swimmers at this meet more often loses than wins. Therefore, it is unlikely that any of them will win.

D. All of Marjorie's cavities are on the left side of her mouth. Hence, she must chew more on the left side than on the right.

E. All of these tomato plants are twice as big as they were last year. So if we grow peas, they will probably be twice as big as last year's peas.

Explanation

Wait. What? This inspector has omitted a prime suspect without any justification. Why couldn't Mr. Tannisch have done it? Since I've spotted the flaw, I'm going to go into the answer choices looking for something that also omits a prime suspect or obvious explanation.

A. Yup. This makes the same stupid flaw. What about the cafeteria food? Why can't that explain why the campers are sick? This answer choice has omitted a prime suspect for the sickness of the campers, so this is our answer.

B. First thought—what does "inclement" mean? Second thought—I don't even see a flaw in this answer choice. Like, yeah, if the two prototypes fair differently in tests, the second might have deviated from the first. Notice that this answer choice doesn't posit that as the only possible explanation, so it's actually fairly reasonable. The answer choice doesn't say that the second prototype did differ in design from the first. Moreover, this answer choice doesn't have the author eliminating a prime suspect without justification. This is out.

C. The flaw here is that just because it's unlikely that each individual swimmer will win, it doesn't follow that it's unlikely no one will win. That's not the flaw we're looking for.

D. Just because all her cavities are on the left side doesn't mean she chews more on her left side. Maybe she drinks pop through a straw every day and has the straw on the left side. Regardless, this isn't the flaw we're looking for. We want the argument to ignore an easy explanation.

E. Not the flaw we're looking for. For the record, this flaw is that just because something happens, for one thing, doesn't mean it will happen for another type of thing. We need to know that the two things in question are similar in some relevant way before we can say whether what happens for thing one will happen for thing two.

That's it. You've just covered all of the "Closed" question types. Hopefully we didn't bore or overwhelm you. Now it's time to get to work. Head to lsatdemon.com and start drilling!

Appendix B:
Open Question Types

Welcome to our Open-question deep dive. As we did in Appendix A, we will explain our process for solving each Open question type. We're going to repeat ourselves a lot, but remember, the LSAT repeats itself all the time.

Weaken

These questions ask you to hurt the main conclusion:

- Which one of the following, if true, most seriously weakens the argument?
- Which one of the following, if true, most seriously undermines the government's claims?
- Which one of the following, if true, most seriously calls into question the conclusion above?

MAKING PREDICTIONS

Because it's impossible to weaken a valid argument, there must be something wrong with this argument. Ideally, you'll have already pinpointed at least one problem when you attacked the passage. But if not, take a moment to find one. Here's how:

1. **Find the main conclusion.**

2. **Find the premises.**
Separate the premises from everything else. After you find the main point, don't assume that all the other statements are premises. They might include an opposing viewpoint, background information, or a concession.

3. **Figure out why the premises don't prove the main conclusion.**
You have to accept the premises as true. But even when you do, they still won't prove the conclusion. Why don't they?

Focus on exactly what the argument is saying to avoid subconsciously helping it. You don't want to make the very assumptions that the test-writers are trying to hide. Your job is to catch those assumptions.

Many arguments, by the way, have more than one problem. The more you notice, the better. But after you spot one or two serious ones, you're ready to read the answers.

CHOOSING AN ANSWER

The correct answer may not necessarily disprove the main conclusion, but it will make that conclusion worse. So as you read each answer, ask yourself:

- Does this answer hurt the main conclusion more than the other four answers do?

Unlike Closed questions, which require you to choose answers based solely on the record in front of you, Open questions specifically ask you what happens when answers are true. They always include language like "which one, if true..." or "which one, if assumed..." So instead of reading each answer looking for reasons why it's not supported by the passage, consider what would happen to the argument if it were true. On Weaken questions, the correct answer provides new evidence that makes you doubt the conclusion without directly contradicting the evidence stated in the passage.

Consider this argument:

> Partner John will be a good fit at our firm because he has worked at two other prestigious law firms.

The correct answer might say something like:

> **B.** John worked at both firms for only two months.

This new evidence doesn't contradict the premises—he still worked at two prestigious law firms—but it does cast doubt on the conclusion that he would be a good fit by raising a potential problem.

Here's another potentially correct answer:

> **C.** John recently broke up with Sally, our firm's managing partner.

Again, this evidence doesn't contradict the premises, but it does cast doubt on whether he's a good fit.

Notice, too, that this answer is unrelated to the original premises; it has nothing to do with John's previous work experience. So don't skip an answer just because it doesn't address the points raised in the original argument. As long as it casts doubt on the main conclusion, it's a possible answer.

If you're debating between two answers that both hurt the conclusion, pick the one that hurts more. That often means choosing the answer that uses stronger wording, such as all or most, rather than some or many. The content of each answer matters much more than the word strength, so focus on the content first. Once you're satisfied that the answer is relevant, then turn your focus to its strength.

Strengthen

These questions ask you to help the main conclusion:

- Which one of the following, if true, most strengthens the argument's overall conclusion?
- Which one of the following, if true, most supports the television executive's argument?
- Which one of the following principles most strongly supports the argument above?
- Which one of the following, if true, most justifies the educator's reasoning?
- The reasoning in the advertisement would be most strengthened if which one of the following were true?

MAKING PREDICTIONS

Because it's impossible to strengthen a valid argument, there must be something wrong with this argument. Ideally, you've already pinpointed at least one problem. But if not, take a moment to find one. Here's how:

1. **Find the main conclusion.**

2. **Find the premises.**

Separate the premises from everything else. After you find the main point, don't assume that all the other statements are premises. They might include an opposing viewpoint, background information, or a concession.

3. **Figure out why the premises don't prove the main conclusion.**

You have to accept the premises as true. But even when you do, they still won't prove the conclusion. Why don't they?

Focus on exactly what the argument is saying to avoid subconsciously helping it. You don't want to make the very assumptions that the test-writers are trying to hide. Your job is to catch those assumptions.

Many arguments, by the way, have more than one problem. The more you notice, the better. But after you spot one or two serious ones, you're ready to read the answers.

CHOOSING AN ANSWER

The correct answer may not necessarily prove the main conclusion, but it will make that conclusion better. So as you read each answer, ask yourself:

- Does this answer help the main conclusion more than the other four answers?

Assume that all five answers are true. The correct answer will give you new evidence that makes you feel better about the main conclusion by fixing, or at least partially fixing, one of the problems you identified.

If you're debating between two answers that both help the conclusion, pick the one that helps more. That often means choosing the answer that uses stronger wording, such as all or most, rather than some or many. The content of each answer, though, matters much more than the word strength, so focus on the content first. Once you're satisfied that the answer is relevant, then turn your focus to its strength.

Test 123, Section 3, Q13

Therapist: Cognitive psychotherapy focuses on changing a patient's conscious beliefs. Thus, cognitive psychotherapy is likely to be more effective at helping patients overcome psychological problems than are forms of psychotherapy that focus on changing unconscious beliefs and desires, since only conscious beliefs are under the patient's direct conscious control.

Which one of the following, if true, would most strengthen the therapist's argument?

A. Psychological problems are frequently caused by unconscious beliefs that could be changed with the aid of psychotherapy.

B. It is difficult for any form of psychotherapy to be effective without focusing on mental states that are under the patient's direct conscious control.

C. Cognitive psychotherapy is the only form of psychotherapy that focuses primarily on changing the patient's conscious beliefs.

D. No form of psychotherapy that focuses on changing the patient's unconscious beliefs and desires can be effective unless it also helps change beliefs that are under the patient's direct conscious control.

E. All of a patient's conscious beliefs are under the patient's conscious control, but other psychological states cannot be controlled effectively without the aid of psychotherapy.

Explanation

This therapist argues that cognitive psychotherapy, which focuses on changing conscious beliefs, is likely more effective than forms of psychotherapy that focus on changing unconscious beliefs. Why? Because only conscious beliefs are under the patient's direct conscious control.

We're asked to strengthen the therapist's argument. Prediction: Psychotherapy is more effective when it focuses on changing beliefs that are under a patient's direct conscious control.

A. This weakens the argument by suggesting that psychotherapy focusing on unconscious beliefs could be helpful.

B. This says that if a form of psychotherapy does not focus on changing beliefs under a patient's direct conscious control, it's difficult for it to be effective. This doesn't say anything about cognitive psychotherapy's effectiveness (which does focus on beliefs under direct conscious control). But it suggests that other psychotherapies that focus on unconscious beliefs are not likely to be effective. Since the conclusion is about the relative likelihood of effectiveness, this strengthens the argument somewhat. This is the correct answer.

C. So what? The argument compares cognitive psychotherapy with forms of psychotherapy that focus on unconscious beliefs. Which one is more likely to be effective?

D. This doesn't affect the argument. For all we know, the forms of psychotherapy that focus on changing unconscious beliefs might also dabble in changing conscious beliefs—that's just not their focus. They could still be just as effective, according to D.

E. Are "other psychological states" under conscious control? And what form of psychotherapy are we talking about here? This is too vague to have any effect on the argument.

Sufficient Assumption

These questions ask you to find an assumption—a missing premise—that, if it were true, would prove the main conclusion:

- Which one of the following, if assumed, would justify the conclusion?
- Which one of the following, if assumed, enables the argument's conclusion to be properly drawn?
- The argument's conclusion can be properly inferred if which one of the following is true?
- The speaker's main conclusion logically follows if which one of the following is assumed?

MAKING PREDICTIONS

A sufficient assumption is an unstated premise that's enough to prove the conclusion. In other words, after you add it to the argument, you don't need to add anything else. The conclusion is now proven. So ask yourself: "What would I add to this argument to fix all the problems and prove the conclusion?"

There's often only one problem because it's hard to write an answer that fixes multiple problems. But if there is more than one problem, the correct answer will fix all of them. If it doesn't, it isn't sufficient.

On that note, if you notice anything in the conclusion that is not mentioned in the premises, then that idea must be addressed by the correct answer; otherwise, that answer will not entirely prove the conclusion and thus be wrong.

Sufficient Assumption questions are among the most predictable questions on the entire LSAT. When the test-ymakers ask you to find something that would "justify the conclusion" or "allow the conclusion to be properly drawn," they mean business. Merely helping the argument is not enough—the correct answer must prove the conclusion. If you're not predicting the correct answer on every Sufficient Assumption question, you're missing a huge opportunity.

1. **Find the main conclusion.**

2. **Find the premises.**
Separate the premises from everything else. After you find the main point, don't assume that all the other statements are premises. They might include an opposing viewpoint, background information, or a concession.

3. **Figure out why the premises don't prove the main conclusion.**
You have to accept the premises as true. But even when you do, they still won't prove the conclusion. Why don't they?

Focus on exactly what the argument is saying to avoid subconsciously helping it. You don't want to make the very assumptions that the test-writers are trying to hide. Your job is to catch those assumptions.

CHOOSING AN ANSWER

If you didn't identify any problems or assumptions, force yourself to go back and find one. There must be at least one. And then, as you read each answer, ask yourself:

- Does this answer prove the main conclusion?
- Does this answer completely fix the argument?

Assume that all five answers are true. The correct answer will give you new evidence that guarantees that the main conclusion is true by completely fixing all the problems you identified.

Because we're trying to prove the conclusion, the stronger the answer, the better. We want the new evidence to be as strong as possible. To be sure, content is more important than word strength, but be wary of answers that use weak words like *some* or *many*. These answers could be correct, but *some* and *many* mean "at least one," which rarely proves the conclusion.

Test 123, Section 2, Q6

An undergraduate degree is necessary for appointment to the executive board. Further, no one with a felony conviction can be appointed to the board. Thus, Murray, an accountant with both a bachelor's and a master's degree, cannot be accepted for the position of Executive Administrator, since he has a felony conviction.

The argument's conclusion follows logically if which one of the following is assumed?

A. Anyone with a master's degree and without a felony conviction is eligible for appointment to the executive board.

B. Only candidates eligible for appointment to the executive board can be accepted for the position of Executive Administrator.

C. An undergraduate degree is not necessary for acceptance for the position of Executive Administrator.

D. If Murray did not have a felony conviction, he would be accepted for the position of Executive Administrator.

E. The felony charge on which Murray was convicted is relevant to the duties of the position of Executive Administrator.

Explanation

The answer to this question, as usual, is to be found in the argument itself. Read carefully. Read slowly. Read it twice if you have to. Go ahead, I'll be here when you come back.

The argument is bad because it assumed (rather than stated) that the position of Executive Administrator is on the executive board.

When I say "assumed," what I mean is that the argument has left out a key piece of evidence. Here, the argument never specifically says that the position of Executive Administrator is an executive board position. Sure, it sounds like it's a board position. But that's not enough. The speaker here needs to specifically state that fact. If it's true, then I think the logic is pretty tight. There's a premise (i.e., stated evidence) that says nobody with a felony conviction can serve on the board. There's a premise that says Murray has a felony conviction. If it's also true that the Executive Administrator is on the executive board, then I would be forced to conclude that Murray can't be on the board.

I haven't even looked at the question yet, let alone the answer choices. But since I now know what the argument is missing, I'm already 90% of the way to answering whatever the question may be.

The question here says "The argument's conclusion follows logically if which one of the following is assumed?" This is what's known as a Sufficient Assumption question. What it really means is "which one of the following would prove the conclusion of the argument?" ("Follows logically" simply means "is proven" on the LSAT.)

I love Sufficient Assumption questions because the answers are really easy to predict. To prove the argument's conclusion, the correct answer simply must cover up the hole in the argument that I have discussed above. The correct answer must somehow connect the position of Executive Administrator to the executive board. Here are a few predictions for what the correct answer might be:

1. "The Executive Administrator is on the executive board." (clean and simple.)
2. "Any job Murray would apply for would be on the executive board." (kind of a weird backdoor, but it would work.)
3. "All jobs in the world are on the executive board." (overkill, but definitely sufficient.)

I think the correct answer is probably going to be something very similar to #1. But I'm not afraid of answers like #2 or #3 here, even though they might seem too strong. Some questions on the LSAT prefer strongly-stated answers. Sufficient Assumption questions fall into this category. It's okay if the correct answer goes overboard here, as long as it proves that Murray can't get the job. Let's look at the answer choices:

A. We were asked to prove that Murray is not eligible for the board. This answer choice couldn't be used to prove that Murray actually is eligible for the board, but that's not the same thing as proving he's not eligible. Furthermore this answer doesn't connect the Executive Administrator position to the board, which is an important connection here. Let's keep looking.

B. Okay, this one would do it. It's not exactly what I predicted, but if this is true, then Murray isn't eligible for the job, and that's what we need to prove. We know he is ineligible for the board because of the felony conviction. If the Executive Administrator position has the same requirements as the board, then Murray is out of luck. Mission accomplished. This is going to be the correct answer. Still, I'll always read the rest of the answer choices, just in case.

C. This answer, if true, makes it easier to get the job, not harder. We want to prove that Murray can't get the job. (Furthermore, it's irrelevant to Murray because he does have a bachelor's degree.) This answer is bad. Very bad.

D. This answer is useless. We're trying to prove that Murray can't get the job, and this answer choice could only be used to prove that he could get the job (if he didn't have the conviction, which he does.) This is a comically bad answer, just like C.

E. No. The "duties" of the position are irrelevant. I suppose this answer choice strengthens the case that Murray shouldn't get the job. (If Murray was convicted of embezzlement, and this is an accounting position, then that would seem to be a strike against him.) But answer B proves that Murray can't get the job. We need to prove our case here, not just strengthen it.

Paradox

These questions ask you to resolve an apparent paradox or puzzling set of circumstances:

- Which one of the following, if true, most helps to explain the apparent paradox above?
- Which one of the following, if true, most helps to resolve the conflict described above?
- Which one of the following, if true, would most effectively reconcile the discrepancy described above?

MAKING PREDICTIONS

The passage rarely has a conclusion or an argument. Instead, it will usually contain two facts that appear incompatible, creating a paradox or mystery.

1. Single out those two facts and find the paradox.
2. Create a why question: Why is one fact happening, even though the other fact is happening?

CHOOSING AN ANSWER

As you read each answer, ask yourself your why question:

- Why one fact, even though the other fact?
- Does this answer explain why X happens even though Y is happening?

Imagine that each answer is true as you read it. Does it scratch the itch created when you read the paradox? The correct answer will give you new evidence that makes you feel better about the mystery by explaining, or at least partially explaining, it.

If you're debating between two answers that both help to explain the paradox, pick the one that helps more. That often means choosing the answer that uses stronger wording, such as *all* or *most*, rather than *some* or *many*. The content of each answer, though, matters much more than the word strength, so focus on the content first. Once you're satisfied that the answer is relevant, then turn your focus to its strength.

Test 123, Section 2, Q25

During the nineteenth century, the French academy of art was a major financial sponsor of painting and sculpture in France; sponsorship by private individuals had decreased dramatically by this time. Because the academy discouraged innovation in the arts, there was little innovation in nineteenth century French sculpture. Yet nineteenth century French painting showed a remarkable degree of innovation.

Which one of the following, if true, most helps to explain the difference between the amount of innovation in French painting and the amount of innovation in French sculpture during the nineteenth century?

A. In France in the nineteenth century, the French academy gave more of its financial support to painting than it did to sculpture.

B. The French academy in the nineteenth century financially supported a greater number of sculptors than painters, but individual painters received more support, on average, than individual sculptors.

C. Because stone was so much more expensive than paint and canvas, far more unsponsored paintings were produced than were unsponsored sculptures in France during the nineteenth century.

D. Very few of the artists in France in the nineteenth century who produced sculptures also produced paintings.

E. Although the academy was the primary sponsor of sculpture and painting, the total amount of financial support that French sculptors and painters received from sponsors declined during the nineteenth century.

Explanation

Here are the facts that we're given in the argument:

1. The French academy of art sponsored painting and sculpture in France.
2. The academy discouraged innovation in art.
3. There was little innovation in nineteenth-century French sculpture.
4. Nineteenth-century French painting showed a remarkable degree of innovation.

So, why is it that paintings showed innovation, but sculptures didn't? Since this is a Paradox question, we want an answer choice that will explain this discrepancy.

- A. This makes zero sense. Why would the sculptures show less innovation if the French academy gave the sculptors less financial support? This fact makes the argument more confusing, so A isn't our answer.
- B. What? This doesn't explain anything. If the individual painters were getting more support than the individual sculptors, how does that explain why the painters kept innovating and the sculptors didn't?
- C. Yep, this explains the argument. The painters could be more innovative because they weren't as reliant on the academy's financial support. This is the right answer.
- D. Ok, but why were the painters able to be more innovative than the sculptors? Answer choice D doesn't explain anything.
- E. So, sculptors and painters both received less financial support in the nineteenth century than they had previously? This doesn't help us make sense of the argument, so answer choice E isn't our answer.

Evaluate

These questions ask you what information would do the most to help you evaluate whether the main conclusion is true:

- Which one of the following would be most useful to know in order to evaluate the argument?

MAKING PREDICTIONS

Because new information couldn't help or hurt a valid argument, there must be something wrong with this argument. Ideally, you've already pinpointed at least one problem. But if not, take a moment to find one. Here's how:

1. **Find the main conclusion.**
2. **Find the premises.**

Separate the premises from everything else. After you find the main point, don't assume that all the other statements are premises. They might include an opposing viewpoint, background information, or a concession.

3. **Figure out why the premises don't prove the main conclusion.**

You have to accept the premises as true. But even when you do, they still won't prove the conclusion. Why don't they?

Focus on exactly what the argument is saying to avoid subconsciously helping it. You don't want to make the very assumptions that the test-writers are trying to hide. Your job is to catch those assumptions.

Many arguments, by the way, have more than one problem. The more you notice, the better. But after you spot one or two serious ones, you're ready to read the answers.

CHOOSING AN ANSWER

The correct answer won't give you new information. Instead, it will ask you what new information you'd like to know.

Because you won't actually get any new information, you won't know whether it will help or hurt the conclusion. But you're looking for the answer that would, if you learned that information, do the most to help or hurt the main conclusion.

So as you read each answer, ask yourself:

- Would the information in this answer either help or hurt the conclusion more than the other four answers?

If you're debating between two answers that could both help or hurt the conclusion, pick the one that could help or hurt more. That often means choosing the answer that uses stronger wording, such as *all* or *most*, rather than *some* or *many*. The content of each answer, though, matters much more than the word strength, so focus on the content first. Once you're satisfied that the answer is relevant, then turn your focus to its strength.

Test 135, Section 1, Q3

Millions of homes are now using low-energy lighting, but millions more have still to make the switch, a fact that the government and the home lighting industry are eager to change. Although low-wattage bulbs cost more per bulb than normal bulbs, their advantages to the homeowner are enormous, and therefore everyone should use low-wattage bulbs.

Information about which one of the following would be **least** useful in evaluating the argument?

A. the actual cost of burning low-wattage bulbs compared to that of burning normal bulbs

B. the profits the home lighting industry expects to make from sales of low-wattage bulbs

C. the specific cost of a low-wattage bulb compared with that of a normal bulb

D. the opinion of current users of low-wattage bulbs as to their effectiveness

E. the average life of a low-wattage bulb compared with that of a normal bulb

Explanation

This argument is contained almost entirely in the second sentence. The logic is simple at its core.

Premise: Though low-wattage bulbs cost more than standard light bulbs do, they come with extraordinary benefits.

Conclusion: Everyone should use low-wattage bulbs.

That's a powerful conclusion. Sure, low-energy lightbulbs might be eco-friendly and save on electricity, but does that outweigh their increased purchase cost? It's hard to say without more info.

Usually, Evaluate questions ask us to find the answer that would be the most helpful in determining the argument's strength. When that happens, we look for a statement that would strengthen or weaken the argument, depending on which way that answer goes.

Appendix B: Open Question Types

On this question, the test is asking us to find the information that would be the least helpful. So the four incorrect answers would help us determine the argument's strength, and the correct answer would be useless.

- A. This would be helpful to know. If the low-wattage bulbs cost more to power, that would weaken the argument. If they cost less, it would strengthen the argument. This information could go both ways, so it would help us evaluate the argument's strength. That means it's the wrong answer since we're looking for a question that wouldn't result in useful information.
- B. The profits of the lighting industry are irrelevant to how much consumers benefit from buying low-energy lightbulbs. This answer won't help us decide if people should replace their regular light bulbs, so this is the correct answer.
- C. How much more expensive is a low-wattage bulb compared to a standard bulb? If the difference in cost is massive, that would weaken the argument. If the cost differential is small, that would strengthen the argument. This would be useful information, so it is incorrect.
- D. This answer is a bit tricky. What does the opinion of lightbulb users matter to the actual benefit of low-wattage light bulbs? I think it is important. What if owners of these new lightbulbs find them to be too dim? Or take forever to turn on? Or the cast light that has a weird, barely-noticeable-at-first shimmer to them that eventually makes you feel like you're about to have an epileptic fit? If that's the case, then the benefits of these lightbulbs decrease. If the bulbs do a great job of lighting houses, then the benefits increase. This would be useful information, so this answer can't be right.
- E. Knowing the lifespan of these new bulbs would certainly help us evaluate the argument. If they last longer than regular light bulbs, that would make them more valuable. If they don't, that would make them less beneficial. This isn't the right answer.

Our answer is B. It doesn't provide any information telling us how valuable eco-friendly light bulbs would be for consumers, so it's the least useful in evaluating the argument.

Appendix C:
Closed Question Types (RC)

Main Point

PREDICTION

- Restate the main point in your head before reading the answers.
- If you need to do so, scan back over the passage to see the big picture.

ANSWER CHOICES

As you read each answer, ask yourself:

- Does this answer match my prediction?

Wrong answers are usually inaccurate or too narrow. An inaccurate answer will often contradict something that was said in the passage or introduce a new idea that was never discussed. An answer that's too narrow will often restate one of the author's premises but not the main point.

When debating two unattractive answers, an incomplete answer is better than an inaccurate one. On the LSAT, inaccuracy is the greatest sin. A complete answer is better than an incomplete one. But incomplete answers can be correct, while inaccurate ones are always wrong.

Supported

PREDICTION

- Treat the passage as evidence or facts.
- Try to figure out what must be true, given what was said.
- If they don't ask you about something specific, it's hard to predict an answer.

ANSWER CHOICES

As you read each answer, ask yourself:

- Does this answer have to be true?
- If not, is it at least the most supported answer?

The correct answer will simply restate something from the passage or infer something that must be true from two or more statements in the passage.

Weaker answers are often easier to prove—*some*, for example, is better than *most*. For more weak words, check out the Word Strength chapter.

Stated

PREDICTION

- Try to remember what the passage actually said.
- If necessary, go back to that part of the passage and reread it.

ANSWER CHOICES

As you read each answer, ask yourself:

- Did the passage say this answer or something very close?

Weaker answers are often easier to prove—*some*, for example, is better than *most*. For more weak words, check out the Word Strength chapter.

Agree

PREDICTION

- Treat the passage as evidence or facts.
- Try to figure out what must be true, given what was said.
- Focus only on what that person believes—ignore what others say.
- The author will often reveal her opinion right after quoting someone else.

ANSWER CHOICES

As you read each answer, ask yourself:

- Does the person have to agree with this answer?

Weaker answers are often easier to prove—*some*, for example, is better than *most*. For more weak words, check out the Word Strength chapter.

Meaning

PREDICTION

- Define the word or phrase in your own words before reading the answers.
- What did the author most likely mean by this word or phrase?
- What word would you use in its place?
- Consider the word in the context of the passage as a whole—not in a vacuum.

ANSWER CHOICES

As you read each answer, ask yourself:

- Does this answer match my prediction?

Wrong answers will often include common definitions of the word that don't match the context in which it was used in the passage.

Tone

PREDICTION

- How strongly does the author agree (or disagree) with this idea?
- Look for words like *fortunately*, *important*, *must*, *claim*, *speculate*, and *incorrectly* in the passage. They reveal the author's attitude.

ANSWER CHOICES

As you read each answer, ask yourself:

- Do *both words* match my prediction?

Evaluate each word separately. In answer (D) below, for example, was Ryder cautious? Yes, okay. But was he neutral? No, he took a side, so this is wrong.

Example:
The passage most strongly suggests that Ryder's attitude toward Gilman's methodology is which one of the following?

- A. disdainful condescension
- B. open dissatisfaction
- C. witty dismissal
- D. cautious neutrality
- E. mild approval

Purpose

PREDICTION

- Describe the *purpose* of the passage, paragraph, or line.
- In other words, what *role* did it play in the passage?

ANSWER CHOICES

Don't look at the answers until you've described the purpose. Then ask yourself:

- Does this answer match my description?
- Does this answer describe exactly what's happening in the passage?

The correct answer describes *why* something was said—not *what* it says.

Organization

PREDICTION

- Describe how the passage is structured in general terms, in plain English.

Example:
The author tells us that some critics oppose construction in the tiger habitat. Then she outlines what the developers plan to do to address those concerns. She ends with reasons why this plan is unlikely to succeed.

ANSWER CHOICES

Don't look at the answers until you've described the passage's structure. Then ask yourself:

- Does this answer match my description?
- Does this answer describe exactly what's happening in the passage?

Read each answer part by part. Pause after each part to ask whether it's happening in the passage.

When you're stuck between two answers, focus on the dissimilar parts.

Analogy

PREDICTION

- Go back and reread the relevant part of the passage.
- Restate how the ideas there relate to each other in general terms.

Example:
Tigers can't use habitats recently occupied by humans because the depleted resources need time to rejuvenate.

General prediction:
Something can't use a place recently depleted of something valuable because that valuable thing needs time to come back.

ANSWER CHOICES

As you read each answer, ask yourself:

- Does this answer describe a *similar relationship*?

Acknowledgements

Ben and I are a couple of dumbasses who got lucky, as our entire team—and anyone who has listened to even a few episodes of the Thinking LSAT Podcast, especially those early ones—is painfully aware. Our mistakes and failures of imagination are legion.

We both wasted three years and tens of thousands of dollars on law school before realizing we would hate being lawyers. We started our own solo LSAT companies as short-term Band-Aids, never imagining they'd become our life's work. Ben wasn't even a podcast listener when we started Thinking LSAT. I thought LSATDemon.com was a bad idea. Fortunately, we're too stupid to fail. We keep trying new things.

Our students, overcoming my and Ben's inadequacies, have humbled us at every turn. They've gone on to Harvard, Stanford, and Yale. They've earned their JDs for free—or even been paid to get them. They've improved their LSAT scores by ten, twenty, thirty, and even forty—yes, 40—points. They're the ones who put in all the work.

Our OG alums are now lawyers, partners, and founders of firms. Someday soon, they'll be congressfolk, judges, ambassadors, senators—and maybe even presidents, for fuck's sake! We are awed by their achievements. This book is dedicated to all of you.

Some of our best alums never even went to law school. They're now better LSAT tutors, writers, and editors than we ever were. Looking at you, Abigail Bradley. Abigail had her hands all over this book, just like everything else we do at LSAT Demon.

Then there's Ryan VanDusen, currently a law student who claims that in another life he'd be a book editor. Based on his success here, I'd say he's a book editor in this life, too. Thanks, Ryan.

Anita Johnson is our endlessly cheery layout wizard. Mahalo, Anita.
Alla Kupriianova gave us this badass cover and keeps our site looking sharp.

Matt DuMont, Erik Johanson, Jenn Haigh, Michael Saxton, and Billy Harrison keep various Demon plates spinning.

To our wives, Maria and Brittany—thanks for putting up with all of this. We know how lucky we are.

We will inevitably forget to name some of the critical contributors to our success—please trust that we know who you are, even if these old guys fail to remember at this particular moment. To our teachers, tutors, writers, the world's best customer service team, software developers, and all our students past and present: the Demon wouldn't be what it is without you. Thanks for helping us keep students from overpaying for law school.

Made in the USA
Middletown, DE
17 May 2025